Dynamic Tao

and
Its Manifestations

To
My wife, Jennie

Dynamic Tao

and

Its Manifestations

A Field Theory Analysis of

Lao-tzu **Tao Te Ching**

道 德 經

By

Wayne L. Wang PH.D.

A *Searching for Tao Series* by

Helena Island Publisher

Published by

Helena Island Publisher
1717 Clemens Road
Darien, Illinois, USA 60561

06 05 04 / 10 9 8 7 6 5 4 3 2 1

Printed in the United States of America

Library of Congress
Library of Congress Control Number: 2003114367

Wang, Wayne L., 1944 -
    Dynamic Tao and Its Manifestations: A Field Theory Analysis of Lao-tzu Tao Te Ching/by Wayne L. Wang;
        p.   cm.
    (A Searching for Tao Series)
    Includes bibliographical references
    ISBN 0-9727496-0-8 (paper back)

    1.   [Tao Te Ching. English]
    2.   Lao-Tzu's Tao Te Ching / translated by Wayne L. Wang,
    3.   Eastern Philosophy and Religion

Cover Graphic: *Holographic Tao Universe* ©2004 by Wayne L. Wang

ACKNOWLEDGMENTS

Never would I have imagined this day that I could share my personal curiosity about Tao Te Ching with you. I truly have gotten much more than what I was seeking. Numerous people have made this happen in a natural way. I need to thank many people I have known in my life.

I remember the simple life of my parents, the kindness of my siblings, and the selfless sacrifices of my brother, Shi-Yuen Wang, to support my higher education. With love, they have shown me a life of simplicity and harmony. Besides this, I was fortunate to have the generous support of Dr. and Mrs. H. C. Liu of I-Lan City, Taiwan, to continue my graduate studies in the U.S. I thank them and their family.

There was no single thread leading to my undertaking of writing this book. Some years ago on a train in Taiwan, I decided to translate this book because it was the shortest Chinese classic and the most difficult book to understand. I spent many long and isolated hours on this book. All my family members deserve recognition for their understanding. In particular, thanks are due to my wife, Jennie, for her encouragement to publish this book. Thanks are also due to my parents who lived in a fashion that was so close to Tao – without ever mentioning the word. I dedicate this work to them, my brother and sisters, my children - Morlie, Steve, Helena, my wife Jennie, and many friends.

I would also like to thank Professors Chen Guu-ying and John Hsueh-li Cheng for their encouragement. Thanks are also due to Rene Dean, Laura Ku, Bill Masters, and Mark Ristich for their comments on the manuscript.

THE AUTHOR

Wayne L. Wang was born in Taiwan and migrated to the U.S. for his graduate studies in engineering and physics. In 1971, Dr. Wang received his Ph. D. degree from Massachusetts Institute of Technology. He did research as a theoretical physicist until 1975, publishing numerous papers on nuclear reaction theory. After spending five years on nuclear reactor safety research, he became a telecommunication engineer specializing in advanced mobile telecommunication systems and data communication.

His cultural background spans equally both the Eastern and Western worlds. The similarities between Tao and quantum physics have attracted his early interest in Tao Philosophy. He believes that Tao is coherent and dynamic, and it may be systematically represented as a modern theory. With his background in the Chinese language and modern physics, he has been able to formulate a Tao philosophy in a most coherent and consistent manner. He introduces a scientific process to formulate Tao Philosophy in a language independent fashion. He has successfully translated the most difficult Chinese classic, the Laotzu Tao Te Ching, with minimum ambiguity.

His first book on this subject, *Dynamic Tao and Its Manifestations*, shows the intimate similarities between Tao Philosophy and Quantum Cosmology. His analysis of Tao Philosophy will set a new framework for modern Tao studies, in both the Eastern and the Western arenas.

Website: http://www.dynamictao.com

For ordering information, updates, and available services, please visit our website or send an email to the author.

PREFACE

All teachings have their principles, and
all efforts have their guiding rules.
Unless by Wu-wisdom[1],
there is no way to understand my principles.

(From the Laotzu Chapter 70)

It is exciting to witness what is happening. The world is marching toward a wonderful spiritual and material unification. Tao philosophers do not have to walk alone. Our understanding of our universe is still developing, but we have enough evidence to be joyful.

It started with quantum mechanics and culminated with quantum cosmology. Within about 100 years, the physicists paved a smooth road for us to understand the ancient Tao philosophy.

Quantum Theory and Cosmology

Einstein received a Nobel Prize for his work on photoelectric effects[2], because he resolved a paradox by observing that light energy is absorbed by atoms in quantized amounts[3] and that a light wave behaves like a particle with energy and momentum. Niels Bohr proposed quantized energy levels for electrons in an atom. In

---

[1] Wu-wisdom is the ultimate wisdom corresponding to the Wu state of Tao. See Section 4.3.

[2] The photoelectric effect was discovered by Hertz in 1887. Einstein's theory referred to particles of light as "light-quanta."

[3] In 1900, Max Planck first postulated that light energy is quantized in small steps because there was a puzzle about heat radiation from a hot iron (black body). He is considered the inventor of quantum theory. Einstein's paper on the photoelectric effect was published in 1905.

1926, Schrödinger proposed a wave equation to describe the hydrogen atom and, one year later, Heisenberg proposed the Uncertainty Principle.

When electrons were shown to produce interference patterns like ripples of waves in diffraction experiments, we had to abandon the particle view as the only view of traditional physics.

But, nothing in nature was changed. We changed and accepted the particle-wave duality. We have accepted the particle-wave duality and the uncertainty principle as nature. In spite of its seemingly contradictory nature, quantum theory became the most successful theory for our microscopic world.[1]

In 1905, Einstein proposed his revolutionary Special Theory of Relativity. We soon abandoned the absolute nature of space and time. Mass and dimensions change with the speed of an object. This mystery replaced many other mysteries. His General Theory of Relativity in 1916 dealt with the gravitational space-time phenomena of the universe. The theory predicted the formation of a black hole, which was then observed.

We have tremendous success in microscopic and macroscopic scales. The physicists started to dream of a unified theory for everything. Quantum Cosmology[2] is such an attempt to unify the quantum theory with general relativity into a unified framework for all fundamental forces known to man. We now have a theory that covers everything from the fundamental particles to the universe.

---

[1] Niels Bohr was awarded the Nobel Prize in 1922. Werner Heisenberg won the Nobel Prize in 1932 for his creation of quantum mechanics. He also worked with Niels Bohr on the Copenhagen Interpretation. Erwin Schroedinger won the Nobel Prize in 1933 for his wave equation. Louis de Broglie won the Nobel Prize in Physics in 1929 for his discovery of the wave nature of electrons.

[2] Quantum Cosmology theorists include the scientists we quote in this book, Stephen Hawking, Peter Higgs, Lee Smolin, L. Susskind, and Gerard 't Hooft. Researches in quantum gravity, particle physics, string theory, black hole thermodynamics (entropy), and loop quantum mechanics lead to an ultimate picture of our universe.

The Ultimate Universe

When we say that we have a unified theory in science, we are actually saying that our minds have been able to re-orient themselves in order to see nature in a unified fashion. Nature has not changed; our minds have changed.

What do we get when we understand the nature of everything? We get a mind that is in harmony with our universe. This is the ultimate universe, inside and outside. Physics describes what we observe outwardly; Tao describes how we observe inwardly. After black hole thermodynamics, superstring theory, loop quantum gravity, etc, Gerard 't Hooft,[1] in 1993, proposed the holographic principle to describe the physical universe which echoes so vividly the way Yo (or *You*) 有 interacts with Wu 無 in Tao philosophy.[2]

Why do we talk about evolution of Physics? Because, in the last 100 years, we have found a way to reconcile our inner universe with our external universe. The story in Physics we are telling our next generation was told once 2500 years ago. In the Tao Te Ching, Laotzu[3] described a Tao philosophical system that today reminds us so greatly of quantum theory and the holographic effects.[4] Our understanding of Physics has evolved to a point where it can provide a consistent way to describe Tao philosophy.

---

[1] Gerard 't Hooft received the Noble Prize in 1999. The holographic principle is described in Section 7.

[2] After holograms were discovered in 1982 in Paris, many areas of research were impacted [see TA92]. It has changed our psychological, philosophical, and religious thinking. The holographic principle helps us interpret Tao philosophy.

[3] Laotzu was believed to be born in 571 BC, the year of the tiger, before Confucius. His surname might have been Lao, instead of Li, which was associated with him by early historians. Confucius twice sought advice from him [WA00]. These facts are subject to endless disputes. Fortunately, this is out of the scope of our interest. As references, we have Laotzu (b. 571 BC.), Confucius (551-479 BC), Socrates (469-399 BC), Plato (427-347 BC), and Aristotle (384-322 BC).

[4] This conclusion was not arrived at by coming from physics to Tao philosophy. We came across Smolin's book [SM01] while this manuscript was near completion. The Preface had to be re-written and a new section was added to discuss the wonderful connections.

Scientific Modeling

We must learn from our physicists how they resolve paradoxes by changing how we think. In order to understand the Tao Te Ching, we have to change how we think. Much of our effort in this work has been to treat the words of Laotzu as the observed Truth and to find meaning in them by re-orienting the way we think.

We have created a scientific model to describe Tao philosophy. After the paradoxes are resolved, we are surprised to see a Tao universe that is consistent with physicists' views of the "physical" universe.

Tao Principles

Our work started as a simple attempt to translate the Tao Te Ching into English. In order to have a systematic approach, we searched for the basic principles of Tao philosophy. We did not expect any connection with modern science.

By careful analysis, the mysteries of Tao revealed themselves, one at a time, and led us to an astonishing conclusion. Tao principles appeared naturally from the Tao Te Ching. We were willingly led by the words of Laotzu, with no intent to mystify or demystify Tao. At the end, we were totally surprised by the *scientific* approach taken by Laotzu.

Why Bother with Tao?

Why is Tao important at all? Tao philosophy can provide a way for those who wish to maintain harmony in the world. Many people believe that Tao is essential in understanding the Chinese culture. If that is the case, it would be a disservice to think that it is mysterious and incomprehensible. It is not particularly useful to consider a culture as mystic. The world has become a global community and we should attempt to understand all cultures on the same footing as our own culture. It is, therefore, important to present Tao philosophy with its utmost authenticity and clarity, as a base for mutual understanding.

The Tao Te Ching

This ancient Chinese philosophy was consolidated by Laotzu 老子 as a book, the Tao Te Ching 道德經, around 500 BC. It is a small book with about 5300 Chinese characters, arranged in 81 Chapters. The verses seem terse, concise, and quite precise. Their suggestive nature has fostered a wide range of speculations and interpretations since the very beginning. Even Confucius expressed his awe about Laotzu.[1]

Chinese scholars debated over its interpretations. As a result, various Tao concepts have permeated into all Chinese philosophical thoughts and Tao became the root of many schools of Chinese philosophy. For unknown reasons, each school speculated on certain aspects of Tao and left other parts as mysteries. These mysteries became the source of fascination about Tao. The Tao Te Ching has since been regarded as a mysterious and self-contradictory philosophical text.

It has become almost impossible to give a fair treatment to Tao philosophy as a coherent philosophical system. The paradoxes are so well accepted that whoever professes a coherent Tao will invite criticisms. And yet, Laotzu firmly stated that his Tao follows certain principles. *Are there really any principles of Tao? What are they?*

Many have attempted to answer this, and many more will try. So far, there has been no sign of convergence in the interpretation of the Tao Te Ching.

Is it a language problem?

Most people have attributed the difficulty of interpretation and translation to the nature of the Chinese language. We, however, believe that the true difficulty resides in not understanding the nature of Tao. Even the Chinese scholars do not have a coherent interpretation of the original text.[2]

It becomes obvious in hindsight that language is not the main problem. We have been able to translate the most difficult concepts and theories in sciences from language to language without loss of

---

[1] Confucius met Laotzu in 501 BC, when Laotzu was 70 year old.

[2] There are 266 known Chinese interpretations listed in [CH00]. There are also numerous translations. For recent English translations of the Tao Te Ching, see [AM03, HE89, WA58, LA92, and KO98].

accuracy. With a coherent Tao philosophy, translation should not be so difficult.

A priori, we have to assume that the Tao Te Ching text is systematic and Laotzu was a coherent philosopher. Both of these assumptions are not obvious, however, and we have to find our evidence in the original words of Laotzu.

In order to resolve the paradoxes and contradictions, we have to find a way to analyze them. In the process of this analysis, we may create and adjust a model of Tao in our minds, in order to accept what we read in the Tao Te Ching. In other words, we have to respect what we observe as Truth and adjust our minds (model) to it. This is similar to the way we solve scientific problems, we create a model or a frame of reference to represent what we observe.

Tao paradoxes exist because we are not synchronized with Tao.[1] We shall show that most of the paradoxes in Tao are the results of our failure to accept what Laotzu has said.

Tao Keywords and Their Relationships

To begin, we have to find a proper frame of reference so we can reconstruct a coherent Tao philosophy. A philosophy is a set of keywords and the networked relationships of these keywords. The translation methodology is to translate the complete set of keywords and to preserve the networked relationships.

Presumably, Laotzu has already defined a complete set of keywords and their relationships in the Tao Te Ching. Some keywords may be obvious, but others may be hidden. For example, Laotzu claimed that we should try to understand his Tao principles with "Wu-zhi 無知.[2]" What is this Wu-zhi? After properly decoding the verses, we recognize Wu-zhi 無知 as a keyword in the

---

[1] When we synchronize with Tao, we re-adjust our minds to synchronize.

[2] Laotzu Chapter 70: Unless by Wu-wisdom, there is no way to understand my principles 夫唯無知也，是以不我知。 This verse has been very puzzling to many because of its Chinese syntax structure. It will remain as a puzzle why these two verses have been hidden from many interpretations. One factor may be that the keyword Wu-zhi 無知 has never been properly identified. The Chinese sentence structure now appears quite straightforward.

Tao Te Ching. As shown in our new interpretation, we have re-discovered Laotzu's concept of Wu-zhi, which was never intended to mean "without wisdom," or ignorance. Instead, it is the true wisdom associated with Wu.

This is an essential keyword that was not properly recognized before. Such a fundamental realization prompted a need to re-analyze all concepts of Laotzu. While we re-interpret or un-interpret the paradoxical verses, we can often recover clear messages of other keywords that have been hidden in the verses.

A Proper Conceptual Language

After we have identified the keywords, we may search for a proper framework to discuss the relationships between the keywords. What is the proper conceptual language for Tao? During our analysis, concepts from modern physics often appear to re-orient our minds to understand Laotzu's words.

We have seen many interesting similarities between Tao philosophy and quantum theory. In quantum field theory, the interaction potential is a result of energy exchange between the two interacting particles. The exchanged energy is quantized and may be represented as *virtual particles*. In our application, we can consider that man-heaven interactions are due to exchange of the Chi energy in the Tao field. We, therefore, find that quantum field theory could be a convenient conceptual language for Tao philosophy.

Laotzu as a Field Theorist

Initially we hesitated to adopt quantum field theory for our discussion, since this is a rather unorthodox approach for Tao philosophy.

We later realized that Laotzu had already formulated his original Tao philosophy as a field theory! He describes the interactions between man and heaven in terms of Chi exchange. With the properties of Chi, his field model shared a common basis with other field theories, such as the quantum field theory.

Why Quantum Field Theory?

Although a few people might consider linking Laotzu's Tao theory to quantum field theory as being unjustified, our view is quite different. The fact that an ancient philosophy can be discussed together with the modern sciences is an important indication of their fundamental truth. We may never know why this is so; but, it would have been a psychological disaster if our spiritual universe were inconsistent with our concept for our physical universe.

We do have a more obvious reason why we can link Tao to quantum theory. For thousands of years, we have been influenced by *dualism*. Soon after Laotzu, Chinese philosophers took on dualistic views on Tao, as shown in their debates on the relationship of Yo 有 [1] and Wu 無 (see Section 6). Even now, we often subconsciously assume dualism in our analysis and we are at a loss when a phenomenon cannot be reduced to dualistic logics. As discussed in Part I, we cannot represent Tao in a purely dualistic framework. Tao is non-dualistic and dualistic at the same time.

Quantum Field Theory of Tao

In early 1900, the physicists were faced with similar puzzling paradoxes and developed quantum theory, as a non-dualistic conceptual language to describe our physical nature. Quantum theory is a coherent framework for discussion of non-dualistic phenomena, and could be a natural candidate for description of Tao philosophy. Physicists have already recognized some physical phenomena similar to Tao, as described by Capra [CA00].

In the course of this work, quantum field theory has helped us to re-orient our minds to establish a conceptual model for Tao philosophy. We stated our hypothesis for a Quantum Field Theory of Tao,[2] and then developed a Tao philosophy based on the words of Laotzu. We will use this as a new conceptual language to describe Tao philosophy.

---

[1] The standard Romanization for the character 有 is *You*, but we have chosen to use *Yo* in this work as a new term to describe an important aspect of Tao philosophy.

[2] We should attribute also the "Quantum" aspect of the theory to Laotzu, since Chi represents minute and imperceptible energies that are imbedded in all under heaven and are exchanged between man and heaven. The symmetry properties of Chi quanta are described by Laotzu as the interplay of yin and yang.

We have also used the results of quantum cosmology to sort out the complicated relationships between Yo and Wu. It was a wonderful reassurance that Tao philosophy is conceptually complete and we can proceed to prepare for the translation.

A Scientific Translation

After we have a coherent model of Tao, we can translate this Tao philosophy into English. As in any scientific translation, we want to preserve the Tao's coherency, by translating both the keywords and their networked relationships. Here we encounter a common problem in any translation - do we have a proper set of keywords in English?

Tao philosophy brings new concepts with it to the target language system. When the target language does not have a proper set of keywords to describe Tao, we have to define new words in the target language.[1] New terms are commonly introduced in sciences and mathematics, to avoid undesirable connotations. After we have selected a complete set of keywords, we can translate Tao concepts and their relationships as a complete model, from language to language.

By analogy to a scientific theory, our representation of Tao philosophy becomes language-independent.

Advantages of a Coherent Model

An advantage of using a scientific model is that its internal consistency can be established among the keywords and their inter-relationships. When we make use of the quantum field theory to develop our description of Tao, we may assume that Chi exchange gives rise to interactions between man and heaven and the characteristics of these interactions will depend on the symmetry properties of Chi.

---

[1] For example, the best translation of the word Tao is simply Tao and, when we attempt to translate Wu 無 as emptiness or nothingness, we introduce unnecessary confusions. In introducing Chinese philosophy to the West, we have already created many new words in English, such as Tao, Tai Chi, Yin, Yang, etc. In our model, we shall add to this list.

We may relate Wu and Yo (mathematically) to the Chi interactions and the bipolar symmetry of yin and yang. This relationship is well understood in quantum field theory and can only be detected in the Tao Te Ching verses with careful observation.

Furthermore, a theory used to correlate what Laotzu said in his Tao Te Ching can also be extrapolated to describe what Laotzu could have said in Tao philosophy. We have already recognized many subtle relationships in Tao that would have been much harder to do without the guidance of a model. Our model may guide us to speculate on other relationships that have not been explicitly articulated by Laotzu!

Laotzu has the Final Words

It is, however, important to point out that the quantum theory is used only as a convenient conceptual language and our Tao philosophy depends only on the words of Laotzu.

Accident is Part of the Design

Near the completion of our work, we discovered some interesting similarities between Tao philosophy and Quantum Cosmology. Tao and physics represent opposite ways of searching for the ultimate truth. It is wonderful to see that they come so close in their conclusions about our universe and our inner universe. Our current understanding of the universe brings new light to our analysis of Tao philosophy, especially the relationship between Wu and Yo.

Our effort has brought us much more than what we hoped to achieve in the beginning - our main purpose was to provide a true and honest translation of the Tao Te Ching. In doing so, we found it necessary to search for a model (to re-orient our minds) for a coherent Tao philosophy. We brought in quantum field theory as a convenient conceptual language, but the resulting revelations soon became a new and revolutionary paradigm for us to appreciate the true mysteries of Tao.

True Mysteries of Tao

We have come to a fuller appreciation of the true mysteries of Tao. The objective of this work is not to remove, or to add, any mystery of Tao. The model clearly shows that we have recovered the true mysteries of Tao and the model will provide a foundation for a new direction of Tao studies. We will have a guiding principle to speculate and extrapolate without going astray.

Great Work as yet Unfinished

This work is clearly not exhaustive and will certainly be refined in further studies. This simple model and its underlying assumptions will certainly not be flawless. We hope that it can help our readers discover new directions for personal interpretations of Tao.

In our analysis, we have sought the Tao principles and the truth in Tao philosophy. We intentionally refrained from addressing historical interpretations of the Tao Te Ching, with exception of some clarifying views by other ancient Chinese philosophers. We have consulted a limited set of reference material so our citation is not inclusive. Various versions of the Tao Te Ching have led to the same Tao principles and dynamics.

We discuss our formulation of the model, *The Dynamic Tao*, in Part I – The Theory of Dynamic Tao.

Our Verse-by-Verse Translation

For the Chinese text, we use the verses of the Mawangdui version as presented by Gao Min [GA96], with exceptions as noted. For historical interpretations by the Chinese scholars, we have consulted two recent Chinese references [CH00, GA96].

We have found that all chapters can be interpreted coherently, within the margin of errors in our interpretations of the ancient Chinese texts. No elaborate speculation is necessary to render a coherent interpretation of each chapter.

Our translation is kept straightforward and accurate in the light of our basic model. We have translated every verse in each chapter in Part II - The Verse-by-Verse Translation.

The original Chinese verses are listed side by side with their corresponding English translations.

Where do we go from here?

This work provides a new paradigm for Tao philosophy, where we can see Tao philosophy in a systematic way. We have reached a new horizon where Tao not only does not mystify us, but can also guide us properly.

This might be the moment, as Laotzu proclaimed in Chapter 72, when the Greatest Tao can enter into our hearts:

民之不畏威，　　*When people have no fear for Tao,*
則大威將至矣。　*the Greatest Tao can enter into their hearts.*

This marks the beginning of a modern era for Tao philosophy.

PART I
THE THEORY OF DYNAMIC TAO

執今之道，以御今之有，以知古始。是謂道紀。

It is by holding the Tao of today to observe
the phenomena of today, that
We come to know its ancient beginning.
It is known as the Threads of Tao.

(From Laotzu Chapter 14)

The Tai-chi Diagram   by Lai Zhi-Te (Ming Dynasty)
太極圖 (明 o 來知德)
One Yin and One Yang is called Tao.
一陰一陽之謂道 (易經)

1

CONTENTS

2

THE THEORY OF DYNAMIC TAO

A Quantum Field Theory of Tao, according to Laotzu

INTRODUCTION

If not ridiculed at, it could not be Tao.

(From Laotzu Chapter 41)

In Part I, we want to present Tao philosophy in a systematic framework with appropriate conceptual language to describe its key concepts and their networked relationships. The Tao principles are based on the words of Laotzu, i.e., the Tao Te Ching 道德經. According to Laotzu, the dynamics of Tao starts with Chi flowing in the universe. This Chi determines the nature of the interactions and the manifestations of Tao. Laotzu describes his model of Tao in an ancient poetic language; we want to decode his principles and present them with minimal personal interpretation.

With his concept of Chi, Laotzu describes Tao with a field theory. He describes the bipolar symmetries in the natural man-heaven interactions. He defined the states of Wu 無, Yo 有, and Oneness as the fundamental states of Tao. He describes the properties of these states and the process of Yo-Wu transmutations in various chapters. The Yo-Wu transmutation process reflects yin 陰 - yang 陽 bipolar transmutation.

As in any field theory, there are laws of interaction. The universal laws of interaction due to Chi exchange may be identified

3

with Laotzu's concept of Te. This is all based on Laotzu's field-theoretic description of his Tao philosophy. We have summarized it as a *Quantum Field Theory of Tao* [WA04].

A field theory is commonly used to describe general interactions in physics, so it is not a surprise to see Laotzu use it as an interaction model.[1] In order to preserve Laotzu's particular concepts of Tao, we find that quantum field theory can provide a convenient conceptual framework. Tao principles are based on the words of Laotzu and Tao philosophy should be independent of the representation framework we choose.

We discuss our modern scientific approach to the ancient Tao and the Quantum Field Theory of Tao in Section 1. The theory is used to analyze Chapter 1 of the Tao Te Ching in Section 2. With great poetic skill, Laotzu describes with only a few verses the complete architecture of Tao in terms of Yo[2] 有, Wu 無, and Oneness 一.[3] Section 3 describes the reverting power and the dynamics of Tao. Our model shows that both Wu and Yo states are critical in Tao philosophy. The Wu and Yo states are then discussed in Section 4 and 5, respectively.

As an integral part of the theory, we have associated Te 德 with the law of man-heaven interactions. This law of interactions applies to both Wu and Yo states, but it is more explicit in the Yo state.

Our model shows a unified view on Wu and Yo. We review the historical debates on Yo and Wu in Section 6. Finally, as a very surprising conclusion, we relate our Tao analysis to the current

---

[1]
In my opinion, Laotzu was the first person to introduce the concept of a field and formulated his field theory of Tao in the Tao Te Ching. He introduced the concept of Chi as mediator of man-heaven interactions. The properties of Chi are determined by its intrinsic symmetry due to yin-yang bipolar interplay. He neutralized the explicit divine power of heaven. The holistic states of the Tao universe are discussed in terms of the harmonious interplay of the states of a system with man and heaven.

[2] We adopted this peculiar English spelling "Yo" for 有, as an attempt to keep it symmetric with the word Wu 無, although Yo is commonly written as "You."

[3]
The Tao philosophical system is clearly defined with only a few Chinese words. The description is so tight that even removal of a few Chinese characters will interrupt its coherence.

4

research in quantum Cosmology, which shows astonishing similarities to Tao philosophy with its Holographic Principle, as discussed in Section 7. We make some comments on Tao philosophy and traditional religions in Section 8. We discuss some examples of our interpretations in Section 9 to show the source of common errors in interpreting the Tao Te Ching and our way to eradicate the paradoxical interpretations. A summary is given in Section 10.

In order to restore the coherency in Tao philosophy, we have identified many fundamental keywords in Tao philosophy. These words are listed here. These terms will be used in our discussion.

Tao 道	The central theme of the philosophical system of Laotzu that deals with the interactions between man and heaven. Tao may be in the state of Yo, Wu, and Oneness, as described in the Tao Te Ching.
Te 德	The (natural) laws of interaction between man and heaven. The guideline for proper actions to achieve harmony in Tao. Te has been translated as the Virtue, Power, etc.
Yo (*You*) 有	The state of Tao that manifests explicitly the laws of interaction for a man to attain harmony with nature. We have chosen to call it Yo (instead of You) as an important technical term in Tao philosophy. It is also phonetically closer to 有.
Wu 無	The state of Tao that manifests as a concealed intrinsic property of Tao. Wu is the base of everything we could know about Tao. Wu and Yo transmutate into each other.
Oneness 一	It is the holistic state of Tao. When Wu and Yo are in perfect harmony, the state of Tao is called Oneness. In this state, man and heaven are one.
Chi 氣	Chi represents energy in the Tao field. The man-heaven interaction is carried by the Chi exchanged between man and heaven.
Tzujan 自然	Tzu-Jan 自然 in Tao Philosophy is often translated as Nature, but it is very different from our usual concept of physical nature. There is no English equivalent.

1   A Modern Approach to Ancient Tao

Tao has survived thousands of years of analysis, remaining as a mysterious philosophy without a modern interpretation. Different schools of Chinese scholars chose to interpret Tao in different ways. Even now, there are few Tao scholars who interpret the Tao Te Ching with complete coherency. Ambiguous understanding of the Tao Te Ching has led to diverging speculations.

In order to make progress in a more systematic way, we need to build a coherent base for Tao philosophy and use it as a common platform to foster further understanding of Tao. Our approach was to start with a few Tao principles and use them to interpret the Tao Te Ching verses. After we understood more about the verses, we then went back to refine our Tao principles.

This process repeated until we established consistency between Tao principles and their interpretations. This process is analogous to what Laotzu describes in Chapter 52:

52　既得其母，　*Once we have some principles,*
　　 以知其子；　*we may investigate its manifestations.*
　　 既知其子，　*After we know its manifestations,*
　　 復守其母，　*we return to abide with the principles.*

This was the "bootstrap" way we started our analysis. We did not start with a pre-conceived theory. We assumed a rudimentary field theory as our reference and analyzed the words of Laotzu until we reached a coherent conceptual framework.

Our purpose was not to give Tao a new interpretation, but to reconstruct the *original* Tao of Laotzu with a modern conceptual theory. Once we are familiar with the Tao principles, the words of Laotzu can be directly appreciated - without the theory. Our modern conceptual representation will also bring to light the relevance of Tao in our modern world.

1.1   WHY MODERN SCIENCES?

Modern sciences represent a break-through in the conceptual limitations of our classical thinking. We need a similar break-through in Tao philosophy.

In the past several hundred years, we have had great successes in the way we adjust to nature, since we have been able to open our minds to accept new and revolutionary scientific concepts. Scientific progress is made within ourselves. We learned how to restore our minds back to harmony with our physical environment.

We may be surprised to learn how much we have changed in the last 100 years. The first elementary particles, electrons, were discovered in 1897, and atomic physics was born. Before 1905, most scientists did not believe in the existence of discrete atoms, but, now, many scientists believe that even space-time continuum has an atomic structure! Our mental attitude towards the world has changed so much. With quantum theory, we are able to accept that an electron can be both a wave and a particle and an electron can interfere with itself to produce ripples. We marvel at a light wave that also behaves like a particle.

Within the last decade, we are willing to accept that there may be no particles at all and everything looks like strings or quantum foams [KA00]. With Quantum Cosmology, we change even more.

In the meantime, Tao is still simply Tao. We have not been able to submit our minds to resolve the mysteries of Tao. We let our minds be immersed in the "assumed" mysteries of Tao. Our understanding of this ancient philosophy has not changed much.[1]

How do we move from here? Can we turn to our modern arena for any experience that we can use to understand the Tao mysteries? Is Tao an ancient philosophy or a philosophy that is still of relevance today? Can we learn from the scientific observations of

---

[1] Tao is certainly more popular in the West compared to 100 years ago. Tao itself has not gained much more popularity in the East, despite its much wider availability. Our understanding of Tao is not better than what we had 2000 years ago - many of our misunderstandings of Tao remain at the same level as those 2000 years ago.

today's world in order to understand our ancient Tao? To this, Laotzu said "yes" in Chapter 14[1]:

14 執今之道，	*It is by holding the Tao of today to*
以御今之有。	*observe the phenomena of today, that*
以知古始，	*we may know its ancient beginning.*
是謂道紀。	*It is known as the Threads of Tao.*

This is a way to say that the ancient Truth should transcend time and, if we observe carefully, we shall see the same threads of truth today. Tao is relevant anytime and anywhere. Modern physics may be one example.

1.2   THE PHYSICS OF TAO

Sciences and Tao philosophy have been kept far apart for a long time and we are still reluctant to admit that science and philosophy should advance hand in hand. As the quantum theory matures, physicists begin to recognize the disappearing boundary between scientific philosophy and Eastern "mystics." For example, Capra describes phenomenon of <u>Tao in physics</u> in his 1975 best seller, *The Tao of Physics* [CA00].

From this side, we see the ultimate <u>physics in Tao</u>. In our efforts to re-construct the Tao philosophy, we have found full dynamics in the words of Laotzu, that we can best describe as *The Physics of Tao*.

Initially, we hoped to use the conceptual languages of modern physics to analyze Tao. Later, we discovered that Tao, as described by Laotzu, is already a rudimentary quantum field theory of today. After this discussion, readers may find that Tao may qualify as an ancient formalism of our modern cosmology.

We have no intention to introduce anything new into Tao. "The physics of Tao" presented itself so naturally in our analysis that we

---

[1]   The interpretations of the words of Laotzu in Part I are slighted modified to merge with the flow of context, so they may be different from the verse-by-verse translations in Part II. They are not extrapolations beyond the Tao principles, which remain unaltered.

were caught somewhat unprepared. Our initial reason to use quantum language was only because our classical language is inadequate to describe Tao. After our analysis, Tao philosophy appeared to be consistent with our current description of our physical universe.

We shall bring concepts of quantum field theory into our discussion of Tao, as illustrations for similar concepts in Tao. Some of these physics concepts are constantly evolving and may have been replaced by even more unified concepts. For our purpose, this is not important at this stage. They are just pointers to what we really need to do - to understand Tao in its original ancient form as described by Laotzu. As physics evolves, our understanding of Tao may also evolve.[1]

1.3   A SCIENTIFIC AND PHILOSOPHICAL ANALYSIS

Why does Tao appear to be so paradoxical and self-contradictory? From our experience in scientific investigations, this indicates that we are using an incompatible frame of reference, or an inadequate language, for our description. In the sciences, we have resolved numerous contradictions and paradoxes just by changing the conceptual language we use in our description of nature.

The conceptual language reflects the way we model nature in our minds. The most obvious ones are in quantum field theory and cosmology. With intensive educational efforts, our ways of thinking have been changed in sciences. We seldom doubt the way nature presents itself. Similarly, we have to change the way we interpret Tao, without changing the words of Laotzu. To resolve paradoxes in Tao, we need to search for a new conceptual framework and a new conceptual language to describe Tao.

Once again, we emphasize that we are trying to re-orient our frame of reference in our minds, so we can see Tao with clarity. We should not interpret Tao to fit our frame of reference. A formal theory will help us re-orient our minds to sort out the complex

---

[1]   There is a possibility that when our understanding of Tao evolves, physics may also evolve. It is interesting to speculate how Tao philosophy could have influenced the development of quantum theory in its very beginning.

dynamic relationships in Tao. Our quantum field theory of Tao is only a model for our minds to synchronize with Tao. It is not a theoretical explanation of Tao.

1.4   THE QUANTUM FIELD THEORY OF TAO

How do we build a field theory of Tao? Laotzu did this by describing the universe as a dynamic system of interactions between man and heaven. Following a field theory formulation, we may have a systematic description of Tao in terms of its key concepts and their relationships, based on the properties of the interaction.

We may summarize Laotzu's field theory hypothesis as:

1. The universe may be represented by a Tao field. This field consists of man and heaven. Tao describes the relationship of man and heaven.
2. The interaction in the Tao field is mediated by Chi 氣, which represents the *quanta* exchanged between man and heaven. Chi exchange gives rise to man-heaven interactions.[1]
3. The law of interactions between man and heaven is called Te 德. Te obtains its inherent properties based on Chi exchange with yin-yang bipolar symmetry.

The above three hypotheses form a simple and powerful field theory of Tao. This is a *scientific* model to describe *The Dynamic Tao*. We may use these hypotheses as the starting point to analyze Tao philosophy in a systematic way.

As an immediate result of the field theory, we have identified the roles of Chi and Te in the Tao philosophical system. As in the quantum theory, Chi is exchanged as quantized *virtual particles* in the Tao field. The relationship between Chi and Te is also well established in the field theory. Therefore, for our purpose, we have

---

[1]   Chi is an ancient concept in Chinese philosophy. It was used also by Guantzu 管子, Hsuntzu 荀子. Laotzu clearly disassociates Tao from divinity and proposed Chi as the driving force for the interactions of man and heaven.

no need to pursue how Chi is quantized and how Te depends on Chi, since physicists have done elaborate analyses already. Behind each phenomenon, there are laws of nature; in Tao, we have Te. We only need to know that the model may be used to describe the interactions and the natural states of the Tao universe.

In Tao philosophy, Laotzu performed such calculations only in his head and described the results in the Tao Te Ching. In Chapter 1, he describes the states of the Tao field in terms of Wu and Yo, and the transmutations between them. In Chapter 42, Laotzu related Chi to the interplay of yin 陰 and yang 陽 and thus, we may deduce the properties of Te from the bipolar yin-yang symmetry. Laotzu describes all the relationships and various states in his book.

As illustrations, we may represent the interaction between man and heaven by the following Feynman diagrams,[1] in Figure 1.

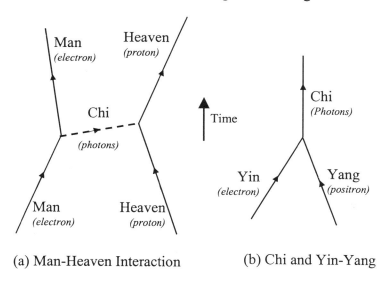

(a) Man-Heaven Interaction   (b) Chi and Yin-Yang

Figure 1   Feynman Diagrams for Chi Exchange

---

[1] Feynman diagrams are used to represent different modes of interactions that appear in the mathematical calculation of the particle interactions. Richard Feynman was an American physicist and Nobel laureate (1965) for his role in the development of the theory of quantum electrodynamics, the study of the interaction of light with atoms and their electrons.

Each Feynman diagram represents an interaction mode and appears as a term in mathematical calculations of the interactions. Physicists often visualize them as physical processes of particle creation and annihilation in the field, although they are not intended to represent actual physical processes.

In Figure 1(a), we show the interaction between man and heaven as exchange of Chi quanta in the Tao field. In this diagram, Chi is generated by man and is absorbed by heaven. Chi may also be generated by heaven and absorbed by man. For comparison, we also show the scattering of electron and proton in an electromagnetic field by virtual photon exchange.

In Figure 1(b), we show how yin and yang generate Chi. When time direction is reversed, it shows how Chi regenerates yin and yang. Laotzu states in Chapter 42 that all beings are endowed with yin and yang, which are blended to generate the harmonious Chi. We also show how this Feynman diagram is used to show that an electron-positron pair may be transformed into a photon.

According to the field theory, the interactions due to Chi will have the bipolar symmetry properties that are intrinsic in yin and yang. Laotzu did not make an explicit statement that Chi is exchanged between man and heaven, but, in Chapter 60, he stated that the laws of interaction of man and of heaven (Te) could be harmonized to guide us back to Tao. From Laotzu's descriptions of man-heaven interactions, it is clear that yin-yang bipolar symmetry is carried in Chi.[1]

1.5 TAO AS A TRADITIONAL PHILOSOPHICAL SYSTEM

In addition to the field theory formalism, it is necessary that Tao philosophy satisfy the requirements of a traditional philosophical system. In order to do this, we have to show that our interpretations of the Tao Te Ching (TTC) display the following characteristics:

1. The TTC verses describe a Tao philosophical system with intrinsic truthfulness, i.e., without contradictions;

---

[1] Later, other Chinese philosophers began to associate Chi with the essence 精 of Tao, supporting the understanding that the Tao field is full of Chi.

2. The TTC describes the entities in Tao philosophy and their relationships; and

3. The TTC contains an ethics associated with the Tao philosophy.

These three requirements are our additional validity checks in our interpretations of the TTC verses. We define truthfulness as the coherency within the model[1] and show that the TTC is internally consistent as to its truthfulness, and that the TTC can be constructed without *apparent* contradictions.

In our analysis, we have shown that the TTC texts are indeed intrinsically consistent and coherent. We have also identified the ethics of Tao philosophy as specified by Te, which represents the proper law of interactions between man and heaven. Having met the requirements, Tao philosophy indeed qualifies as a traditional philosophy.

1.6   WHY DO WE NEED A COHERENT TAO?

Our purpose is to describe Tao and to translate the Tao Te Ching. We need a self-consistent description of Tao before we can translate Tao philosophy without distortion. To be more explicit, our minds should be in a coherent frame of reference before we can translate Tao with consistency. Further systematic progress can be made only when we have a coherent frame of reference.

In any philosophy, there are keywords and networked relationships. The main purpose of developing a coherent model of Tao is to identify all of its key concepts and to understand their relationships. This is a requirement for any scientific modeling.

Laotzu has already defined the necessary keywords and described their networked relationships in the Tao Te Ching. Our

---

[1] As defined in [SA96], "Coherence refers to a systemic consistent explanation of all the facts of experience. To be coherent, a person must arrange all pertinent facts so that they will be in proper relationship to one another consistently and cohesively as parts of an integrated whole. Whatever facts are brought to light must be explained, must somehow be fitted into the system as a relevant or integral part."

challenge is to recognize such a complete set of keywords and to re-construct their networked relationships.

After we have a coherent description of Tao, its intrinsic properties can be preserved in the translation and interpretation.

1.7   A LANGUAGE-INDEPENDENT MODEL

Our initial reason for choosing a scientific model[1] was driven by the dynamic nature of Tao. It is also convenient because most people are somewhat familiar with modern sciences.

After our analysis, we realize that there is another critical reason to have a scientific model: a scientific model makes Tao philosophy culture-independent. Therefore, our model for Tao will be language-independent. This is important for a successful translation and will require less ambiguous personal speculations.

The scientific concepts we use are also well defined and language-independent. We do not need to coin elaborate new terms in our discussions. Their descriptions are readily available in most languages and well presented.[2]

---

[1]   We define a scientific model as a model with internal coherency. A scientific model is proven "correct" only by its consistency. For Tao philosophy, the model is "correct" when it renders coherent interpretations.

[2]   For example, scientific terms are available in most languages on the Internet.

2   The Architecture of Tao Philosophy

Before Tao, the universe was formless and chaotic. Man had no notion of heaven and earth. When Tao was bestowed upon the universe, the universe became conscious and assumes certain intrinsic order. Laotzu describes this universe in terms of Tao.

Since the beginning of the conscious universe, all emptiness has been filled with the primordial Chi. Heaven and earth evolve with Tao and all are in harmony with Tao. This Tao universe may be described in different states. The states are dynamic and evolve with an internal rhythm.

Laotzu describes the architecture of Tao in Chapter 1, which is a very concise and powerful proclamation of the Tao universe.[1] We may depict this Tao universe in Figure 2.

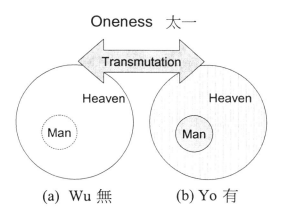

Figure 2   Architecture of Tao Universe

In this architecture, Tao is described in terms of its two fundamental states as Wu 無 and Yo 有. These two states are

---

[1]   Laotzu used only four verses to define the architecture of Tao, and another three verses to describe the states and transmutation of Tao. Parts of this short chapter had been puzzling to us, which, we understand now, was due to improper interpretation.

15

transmutated with each other, to form a unified state, which is called the *Ultimate Oneness* 太一 state. The Oneness state shows the relationship between Wu and Yo states. Laotzu defines Oneness only implicitly by saying that Wu and Yo come from the same source. This architecture is explicitly described by Chuangtzu as, "Tao is built upon constant Wu and Yo, and mandated by Oneness."[1] Laotzu describes these two fundamental states as follows.

In Figure 2(a), man is one with heaven. All interactions with heaven are *implicit* to man. Man and heaven are indistinguishable. In this state, man is *sub- or un-conscious* of any interaction with heaven because he is totally one with heaven. It is called the Wu state. In Figure 2(b), man becomes *conscious* of the interactions with heaven and will observe the *interactions* between man and heaven. Man in this state is still totally synchronized with heaven. The interactions appear *explicit* to man, so it is called the Yo state.

These two states constantly transmute into each other. We shall show how Laotzu describes these two states in Chapter 1.

2.1   PROCLAMATION OF TAO

We often believed that it is difficult to describe Tao.[2] However, Laotzu has described a complete Tao philosophy in the Tao Te Ching. In Chapter 1, we shall witness Laotzu's astonishing ability for clarity and simplicity.

The first verse is the most familiar one in the book. This verse is a powerful preamble of Tao philosophy. We interpret it as a simple and positive statement about Tao:

---

[1] 莊子：「建之以常無有，主之以太一。」Chuangtzu describes the Oneness state by saying "in the grand beginning, there are Yo and Wu 泰初有無 and Wu and Yo are un-manifested 無有無名; It is the source of Oneness 一之所起. Oneness state manifests without form 有一而未形" We may also equate Tao as the Oneness, as Huainantzu 淮南子 stated, Tao (Oneness) is substantiated by Wu and Yo 道以無有爲體。Lie Tzu 列子 had a similar description: "In the state of Greatest Oneness (Change), Chi is not displayed 太易者，未見氣也. In the Greatest Beginning (Yu), it begins with Chi 太初者，氣之始也."

[2] Chuangtzu 莊子 also stated in Chapter 25 "Tao is beyond description, with or without words 言、默不足以載"

道、可道也，　　*Tao may be spoken of, and it is*
非恒道也；　　　*not a constant Tao.*

This interpretation reflects quite accurately the spirit of the original Chinese text.[1] Unfortunately, this verse has often been interpreted negatively as "The Tao that can be told is not a constant Tao." This negative statement invokes a mystic feeling, but it has also misled many.

The second part is a simple declaration that Tao is not static. The relationship between man and heaven is dynamic. In Laotzu's descriptions, it is a *Dynamic Tao*. The fact that Tao may be described should not reduce its mysteries. Our analysis will identify clearly all mysteries of the dynamic Tao.

The next verse is related to the concept of Tao and its manifestations. The concept itself is often called the *Ming* 名 in Chinese philosophy. Its corresponding manifestation is commonly called the *Shih* 實. The *concept* can be described through its manifestations. Laotzu proclaims the *Ming* of Tao in the second verse as,

名，可名也，　　*This (concept) may be manifested, and it*
非恒名也。　　　*is not a constant manifestation.*

Literally, we have, "Its *Ming* can be *ming*-ed, and it is not an unvarying *Ming (Manifestation)*." Lao-tzu used the first *Ming* for the abstract concept of Tao, the second *ming* as a verb, to manifest, and the third *Ming* as a noun referring to the manifestation.

---

[1] The Wang Bi 王弼 version 道可道非常道 has led to many interpretations that claim Tao is indescribable. Despite this popular interpretation, there is no indication in the original Chinese text that Tao is beyond description. We may even interpret 道可道 as "Tao may be used to guide us," by recognizing the second 道 as to guide.

This interpretation is echoed by Hsuntzu : "After *Ming* is fixed/established, the manifestations appear in many different ways."[1]

2.2   THE STATES OF TAO

After the short proclamation, Laotzu continued to define the manifestations of Tao. Laotzu describes the initial state of the Tao universe in Chapter 25, as "with chaotic substance, it exists before heaven and earth."

When Tao is bestowed, the universe is in the Oneness state and becomes "ever evolving without an end, becoming the mother of heaven and earth." Therefore, in the very beginning, there was Tao in the universe.[2] This Tao universe is dynamically manifested in two states: Wu 無 and Yo 有.

2.3   THE WU STATE 無

The Wu state shows the intrinsic harmony of man and heaven. This state is inherently difficult to describe since man is merged subconsciously with all beings and with heaven and earth. However, Laotzu has characterized this state in many chapters of his book.

Laotzu defines this state as from where everything begins. He states:

無、 *As Wu,*
名萬物之始； *it marks the beginning of all beings;*

This verse may be interpreted as *All beings begin in the Wu state.* Wu is an incipient state, in which all beings are concealed.

The Wu state is filled with Chi and it is not empty. Tao field changed emptiness into virtuality. Laotzu describes it as a state of

---

[1]   Hsuntzu Chapter 22 Rectifying Name 荀子《正名》：名定而實辨.

[2]   It is interesting to note that Heidegger asked, "Why are there beings at all instead of nothing?" [HE00] There seems to be some interesting relationship between our philosophical analysis of Tao and modern philosophy of Heidegger.

virtuality 虚. The chaotic universe becomes orderly in this state. We may call this field, a *Virtuality Field* 虚場.[1]

We have identified Wu as a state.[2] The Wu state represents unconscious harmony with the whole Tao universe. We may figuratively describe this state as a man-heaven *resonance* state. Man is *resonating*, and becomes one, with heaven and earth.

Laotzu describes the Wu state in Chapter 4, 5, 6, 10, 14, 16, 21, 25, 32, 34, 35, etc. Laotzu often showed both Wu and Oneness states in the same chapter.

The subconscious Wu state cannot be described in detail, since whatever we can describe in detail will transmutate into the consciousness of the Yo state. This is emphasized by Laotzu in Chapter 67, where he said that Tao could not resemble anything describable, as Tao is always linked with the Wu state.

2.4   THE YO STATE 有

Laotzu describes the Yo state with more details in the Tao Te Ching. In the Yo state, we turn on our *consciousness* to be aware of our interactions with heaven. The Yo state represents what we can "see" in Tao.

Therefore, in the Yo state, the individuality of all beings is manifested and all interactions become *conscious processes*. In other words, we may say that this self-consciousness brings all beings into being. So Laotzu states that:

---

[1] There is an extremely similar and interesting phenomenon in modern physics. Originally, all particles have no mass. After mysterious field strength is imposed, all particles obtain their specific masses. This field is called "the Higgs Field" in physics. The Higgs field is very simple and is indistinguishable from empty space. We shall call this field simply as the "Virtual field 虚場" of the universe, since it is quite similar to the "virtuality 虚" state of the Tao field. The Higgs bosons were postulated by 't Hooft and Veltman (1999 Nobel Prize winners) and are being pursued eagerly in Particle Physics experiments planned for the year 2005.

[2] Most other interpretations and translations have followed Wang Bi and treated Wu as an adjective, so Wu-Ming 無名 is taken to be the Un-named or the Nameless. Our interpretation is in line with the interpretation of Wang An-Shi 王安石 (1021-1086).

有、	*In the Yo state,*
名萬物之母。	*it is the mother of all beings.*

The process in the Yo state will guide all beings to live in harmony with heaven. We may say that, *"Yo fosters the consciousness of all beings."*

The Yo state is governed by explicit rules of interaction in order to maintain harmony between man and heaven. Laotzu often describes this in terms of Te or the reverting processes of Tao. We may envision that the Yo state is the manifestation of Tao to man as an observer. We may figuratively say that, in the Yo state, we are in *synchronization* with heaven. Heaven interacts with man via this synchronization signal. In this synchronization process, heaven may provide different rhythms to all beings.

Laotzu describes the Yo state in Chapters 2, 3, 9, 12, 24, 27, 28, 30, 31, 38, 46, etc. These are only examples. The Yo and Wu states are often not clearly distinguished in a chapter. However, the actions of the Sage are always examples of the proper actions in the Yo state.

We should also point out that Tao manifests in different ways in the Yo states to different observers. But, all manifestations will be consistent, because there is only one Tao universe.[1] This means that the interactions may change under different conditions, but the fundamental laws of interactions remain the same. We shall discuss this further in Sections 3.4 and 7.

2.5   TRANSMUTATIONS OF WU AND YO

We now come to a unique phenomenon in Tao. The two fundamental states Wu and Yo are not independent. They are always coupled and active simultaneously at all times.

This important coupling is due to the reverting power of Tao and is described by Laotzu in the next two verses.

---

[1] In quantum cosmology, this is called a context-dependent theory where there is only one universe and each observer (with context) sees different but consistent descriptions of the universe [SM01].

These verses have been punctuated in two ways.[1] After careful considerations, we have concluded that Laotzu introduced his concept of *transmutations* of Wu and Yo in these verses. This will become more evident later in our discussion. The first verse may be interpreted as:

恒無、欲　　*As constant Wu, it is to show*
以觀其所妙；　*its display of minute appearance (into Yo).*

While the Tao universe is in the true, or constant, Wu state, it shows the mystery of its transmutation into the Yo state. Laotzu describes this process of minute manifestation of Yo as 妙.[2] We may also say that Tao always remains in the Wu state in order to display how the Yo state comes into being. This is a picture of the mysterious germinating process, by which the Yo state emerges from the Wu state. Wu contains *coded within it* information about its relationships to Yo.[3]

Similarly, when Tao is manifested in the Yo state, we may observe how Yo disappears (transmutates) into Wu. This next verse may be interpreted as:

---

[1] We are fully aware of the most popular interpretations, following Wang Bi, by parsing the verse as 無欲 and 有欲 (without and with *desires*). We have chosen our punctuation to show the critical importance of Wu and Yo and their transmutations in Tao Philosophy. We deem that the punctuation used in Wang Bi (about 200 A.D.) and Hoshangkong 河上公 (179-159 B.C.), or more explicitly in Mawangdui text (about 200 B.C.), was an error introduced not long after the verses were written by Laotzu. We support the punctuation proposed by Wang An-Shi. The phrase 恒無 appears consistently in Chapter 1, 32, and 34.

[2] *Miao* 妙 is ultimate minuteness. Wang Bi said, "The word *miao* means the ultimate minuteness 妙者，微之極也。" We may also note that some ancient texts use the word for mystery as 眇, which has an eye 目, as to observe.

[3] This is a paraphrase of Smolin's description of cosmological holograms, "The world must be a network of holograms, each of which contains coded within it information about relationships between the others." [SM01] This is discussed in Section 7.

恒有、欲　　　　*As constant Yo, it is to show*
以觀其所徼。　　*its display of disappearance (into Wu).*

When Tao universe reaches its true, or constant, Yo state, we see how the Yo state disappears and transmutates into the Wu state. Laotzu describes this process of disappearing as 徼.[1] There is always a germinating seed of Wu in the Yo state, i.e., Yo contains *coded within it* information about its relationships to Wu.

The importance of the above two verses is in the transmutation process of both Yo and Wu states into each other. Tao does not simply switch between two independent states; it reverts between the Yo and Wu states, via its reverting process discussed in Section 3.2. This process is also the base for mutual transmutations of Yo and Wu 有無相生, which will be discussed in Section 3.6.

2.6   DUALITY OF TAO

The two states, Wu and Yo, are a result of the same interactions of Chi exchange between man and heaven. Therefore, they are from the same source. They are *simultaneously* the manifestations of Tao. Both states describe the same Tao. This is the *duality* of Tao.

Laotzu describes this duality of Wu and Yo in the following extremely concise verse:

兩者同出，　　*The two emanate from the same;*
異名同謂。　　*they are different descriptions of the same.*

Both Wu and Yo states are from the same source, and they are different manifestations of the same descriptions (of the same Tao). This verse is an extraordinary example of the conciseness of Laotzu's words. This verse implicitly, yet unambiguously, introduces the concept of *Oneness*.

---

[1] *Jiao* 徼 is the end, return or concealment. Wang Bi said, "The word *Jiao* means the end or return 徼，歸終也。"

We have identified the "two" as Wu and Yo from the same source. They are different manifestations to describe the same Oneness.[1] Wu and Yo are thus defined as the two simultaneous manifestation modes of the same Tao.[2] There is only one Tao. The Oneness state will be described in Section 7.4.

2.7 MYSTERY AND GATEWAY TO REVELATION

Which state is the core of Tao philosophy? In the light of our theory, this question does not arise, as both Wu and Yo are the core of Tao philosophy simultaneously.

Laotzu declared both states to be *profound*. They are both the gateway to all revelations to all mysteries. Therefore, Laotzu states:

玄之又玄，　　*They are profound and profound, and*
眾妙之門。　　*are the gateways to all mysteries.*

This is to emphasize the important roles of Wu and Yo in the mystery of Tao. Both Wu and Yo are profound. All mysteries may be understood in terms of the relationship between Wu and Yo.

2.8 THE DYNAMIC TAO

In a single chapter, Laotzu provided a concise and exact description of the dynamics of Tao. It requires very little additional support from other chapters for its completeness, except in Chapter 42, where Laotzu explicitly linked Tao to Oneness and identifies the harmonious Chi as the source of harmony.

Chapter 1 sets the stage for a very dynamic Tao. Throughout the book, Laotzu describes the properties of the states of Wu and Yo

---

[1] It is interesting to compare this to the particle-wave duality of an electron in quantum theory. The interplay of Wu and Yo is not that much more beyond our imagination.

[2] In the Wang Bi version, this verse has some variation as, "The two are from the same source and have different manifestations 兩者同出而異名. Both are mysterious 同謂之玄。" This variation has no impact on the principles of Tao. The Mawangdui version seems to be more concise.

and their relationships through his concept of transmutations. The utmost state of Tao is the Oneness state where Wu and Yo achieve their ultimate balance.

It is interesting to summarize this by calling this Tao: *The Dynamic Tao*.

the step to the left - alternating with a step to right
points to the swing - to the dynamical features
always in change for adapting and finding the best response
always in change between energy and matter too

(Tao [1])

Description of the Sinograph of Tao by Wulf Dieterich

---

[1] The above symbol is an ancient Sinograph for the Chinese character Tao.

3   The Characteristics of Tao Dynamics

The reverting action of Tao is critical to coordinate the harmonious relationship of Wu and Yo to maintain the Oneness state. Tao always reverts Wu into Yo and Yo into Wu, via the mysterious mechanism of transmutations.

This process is of such fundamental importance that Laotzu included it in Chapter 1. The interplay of Wu and Yo are described in many chapters, such as Chapter 22, 28, 39, 40, etc.

In the Oneness state, our minds are always in total harmony with heaven,[1] with the reverting power of Tao maintaining the Oneness state. When we lose our harmony with heaven, the reverting power appears to act as a re-synchronization signal for man to return to harmony. Man should constantly seek such *re-synchronization* with heaven.

3.1   DEVIATION OF MAN'S MIND

What is the source of our deviation from Oneness? Laotzu attributed such deviations to "our minds," which makes our Chi strong. In Chapter 55, we have:

55 心使氣曰強 *Driving Chi with our minds leads to strength.*
物壯則老， *Showing strength leads to decay.*

When we are driven by our minds, we will lose harmony with heaven and we become weak. Laotzu describes such deviations from Oneness as unstable, and Tao will guide man back to Oneness.

When strong Chi is present, we are in a "limited" Yo state. Laotzu has described these limited Yo states as the deviated or the

---

[1]   Our minds are always active in the Oneness state with Tao. When we are with the Wu state, we are also active with a Wu-mind 無心, which is discussed in Section 4.7. When we are in the Yo state, we are still in harmony with heaven and do not deviate from Tao. When we deviate from Oneness or Tao, we mean that we are unable to maintain our synchronization with heaven. When we deviate very far from Oneness, we are in the lost state.

lost states. However, Laotzu is an optimist and believes that man can always recover from the deviated states by following Tao.

To eliminate strong Chi, we have to subdue our minds and synchronize with Tao. Laotzu describes this in Chapter 48, as shedding our desires and actions until we can act according to the Wu state:

48 　損之又損， 　　*By shedding upon shedding,*
　　以至於無爲。 　*until we attain state of Wu-action.*

Here we have interpreted Wu-wei 無爲 as the proper actions according to the Wu state (or the Oneness state) as discussed in Section 4.2. Once we are in harmony (synchronization) with heaven, we will automatically rejoin the Oneness state.

3.2　THE REVERTING POWER

The reverting power originates from bipolar interplay of yin and yang, which is the basic reverting transmutation mechanism in Tao philosophy. Yin-yang transmutation gives rise to Yo-Wu transmutation.

Laotzu called this the reverting power in Tao. We are always in the Tao field and there is always an active background reverting power of Tao. Laotzu proclaimed this in Chapter 40:

40 　反者 　　*Reverting (back to Oneness) is*
　　道之動； 　*the way Tao moves.*

This reverting power is active under all conditions, including the Yo and Wu states, and also the deviated and the lost states. It acts as a synchronization signal for man. This reverting action is the way Tao restores everything back to the state of tranquility.[1]

---

[1]　In the movement of a pendulum, the force acting on the pendulum is always in the direction against its displacement from the equilibrium state, which is the center point. Any movement towards either side will induce a reverting force

Laotzu describes this reverting process in many ways. When we are in a deviated state, or in a lost state,[1] the reverting power acts as a guiding light for man to return to Oneness. Laotzu describes this in Chapter 52:

52	用其光，	*Following its light,*
	復歸其明，	*we return to its enlightenment.*

We see the *light* as the synchronization signal in the Yo state, and the *enlightenment* as the Oneness state. Wentzu also made a similar statement to this effect: "The leader upholds the enlightenment and the people will follow its light."[2]

3.3 ALL-ENCOMPASSING POWER

Tao works in all situations and its reverting power is active in all states of man-heaven relationship. This is an important characteristic of compassion in Tao. There are many examples for this all-encompassing nature of Tao in the Tao Te Ching. Laotzu states in Chapter 27, 62, and 71, that

27	物無棄材，	*Being receptive to all, without abandoning*
	是謂襲明。	*any, is to Follow (true)Illumination.*
62	人之不善，	*If people can not master (Tao),*
	何棄之有。	*how can we just abandon them?*
71	聖人之不病，	*The Sage shows no sickness (dislike).*

To illustrate Tao's compassion, we use the following extreme example to show how Tao will recover a man from the lost state.

---

towards the center. The state of equilibrium is the Wu-state and the reverting power is the interplay of yin and yang.

[1] We may say that a lost state is some state that is far from the Oneness state. The reverting power of Tao is still active in the lost state. Laotzu describes this in Chapter 23.

[2] Wentzu 文子: 上執大明，下用其光.

Laotzu describes this extreme case in Chapter 23,

23 失者　　　*While one is in a lost state,*
　　同於失。　*one should synchronize with the lost state.*

　　同於失者，*For those synchronized with the lost state,*
　　道亦失之。*Tao will work (effectively) in the lost state.*

When we are in a lost state, we first have to recognize that we are in the lost state, and then Tao will work effectively in the lost state.

The important thing is that we have to recognize that we are in the lost state and synchronize to it, before Tao can be effective. We may extrapolate this to mean that the reverting power is only effective when we are in a state of synchronization with heaven. This state may not be the Oneness state, but it could be one of the many Yo states. The reverting power of Tao will expand our limited view in a Yo state to a full-view of the Oneness state.

Laotzu never abandons any of these states, as he explicitly stated in Chapter 23 and 62.

This all-encompassing reverting power of Tao is also reflected by the fact that Laotzu always suggests ways to recover. In Chapter 18, we have:

18 故大道廢，*When the Great Tao is ruined,*
　　安有仁義。*benevolence and righteousness will appear.*

This is an indication that benevolence (Jen) and righteousness (Yi) will appear as the proper ways to recover from the lost state. We have identified Jen and Yi as the next-level recovery efforts. They are also different manifestations of Tao. Tao will appear as different (Yo state) manifestations to each lost man. Even Sages will apply different actions in different states, as stated by Wentzu that *Sage's laws change with situations.*[1]

This concept is important when we interpret the Tao Te Ching.

---

[1]　Wentzu 文子: 聖人法與時變 [WA00]

3.4   THE UNIVERSAL LAWS OF INTERACTION

What do we mean by dynamic manifestations of Tao? What do we mean by there are *many* Yo states, when there seems to be only one Wu state?

From the descriptions in Chapter 18, 23, 38, 54, 61, etc., we may identify this important property of the Yo state. When we are in the Yo state, each person may see a different Yo state of heaven and try to synchronize to it.[1] For Tao to be effective, each man should always synchronize with the heaven he can see. In other words, the synchronization is dynamic, although the law is universal.

In our field theory, the law of interaction is based on the properties of the Chi exchanged. Laotzu called this law of interaction as Te 德 in Tao philosophy. In each Yo state, man will only be able to perceive a limited scope of laws, so Te may appear to different observers as different sets of laws.

The appearance of Te depends on the scope we have. Laotzu gave an example in Chapter 54, where Te has different qualities in different environments, such as in self, a family, a village, a country, or the world. There are different proper actions in each environment. Laotzu gave an example for a large and a small country according to Tao in Chapter 61.

So we can see that Te is not a fixed manifestation; it is dynamic. Laotzu describes the changing levels of Te in Chapter 38. There is a hierarchical structure of the manifestations of Te for people in different states. After we lose Te in the Oneness state, we have Jen 仁, Yi 義, and Li 禮。These states of Jen, Yi and Li are still part of the realm of Tao and should not be regarded as deviation from Tao.

3.5   THE HARMONIOUS CHI 氣

We now come to the origin of Tao dynamics – and see why the reverting power of Tao has such a unique property. We can derive

---

[1]   This is because man is not outside the system. In quantum cosmology, this is called a Context-dependent theory, where Context refers to the state of the observer [see SM01]. Various heavens perceived by individuals are consistent since they are different descriptions of the same heaven. See Section 7 for further discussion of holographic principle.

the properties of the states from the characteristics of the Chi quanta in the Tao field.[1] Chi quanta retain specific built-in symmetry of yin and yang, so that the resulting interactions and the states will have similar symmetry properties.

Chi plays a critical role in the dynamics of Tao, as shown in the characteristics of the reverting power to maintain the state of harmony with Oneness. Despite its vital role in Tao, Laotzu introduced Chi in a single verse in Chapter 42:

42 萬物負陰而抱陽 *All beings carry yin and embrace yang, and*
　　沖氣以爲和。　　*blend them into Chi to achieve harmony.*

Chi appears again only in Chapter 10 and 55. The origin of the symmetry in Chi is from the bipolar symmetry of yin-yang interplay and we call this Chi the Harmonious Chi 和氣.

Chi is active in both Wu and Yo state. The property of Chi is reflected in the properties of man-heaven interactions.

3.6   WU-YO TRANSMUTATION 有無相生

It is clear by now that the relationship between Wu and Yo is complicated. It has been a topic of many debates in Chinese philosophy. Our model should provide a unified framework that can delineate the relationship between Wu and Yo.

Wu and Yo are always in a state of mutual transmutation. They are coupled in a rather unique way, which is the base of Tao philosophy. Laotzu has indicated this process of their transmutations in Chapter 1. He formally declared this transmutation process in Chapter 2 as:

---

[1] In a field theory formulation, we have defined Chi as the energy, or quantum virtual particle, exchanged between heaven and man. Chi is both energy and matter, as these two are indistinguishable at the range of our minute amount of energy and infinitesimal time scale. It is interesting to quote Zhang Dainian [ZH02]: "Perhaps the best definition of the Chinese word Chi 氣 (qi) is provided by Einstein equation, $E=mc^2$."

30

2　有無相生　*Yo and Wu come into being in each other.*

We may say that Yo and Wu bring each other into being. This relationship originates from yin-yang bipolar symmetry, where we may say that *yin and yang come into being in each other*. Because of this intrinsic property, we cannot have a concept of a *pure* Yo state or a *pure* Wu state. These two states are always *superimposed or entangled*. This effect will be discussed later in this section.

This nature of *superposition* goes beyond the paired dyads. We may see such superposition in Chapter 42, where the three states are inter-related in the same way:

42　道生一，　　*Tao brings Oneness into being.*
　　一生二，　　*Oneness brings Two into being.*
　　二生三，　　*Two brings Three into being.*
　　三生萬物。　*Three brings all-beings into being.*

To be consistent in the superposition property, the *order* of creation is irrelevant. The relationship is cyclic, so all-beings return to Tao. There is no causation among these states. All states are parts of Tao. Such cyclic transformation is allowed in quantum theory, if the process preserves the symmetry properties.

The creation process of each state from the superimposed state or from each other may be speculated, but will probably never be resolved.[1]

3.7　YO-WU ASYMMETRY

What are the symmetry properties in the Yo-Wu relationship that should be preserved in our interpretations of Tao philosophy?

---

[1] In today's Physics, we are still puzzled with creation of particles from the vacuum. Discovery of a dynamic vacuum was a major progress in modern physics. It is interesting to note that a similar paradox in quantum mechanics exists: a wave function (un-manifested) may collapse to show the property of a particle (manifested). This process is accepted with what is called "the Copenhagen Interpretation" of quantum theory.

In the Tao Te Ching, there is only one other verse dealing directly with the relationship between Yo and Wu. In Chapter 40, Laotzu said,

40 有生於無   *Yo comes into being in Wu.*

Many interpreters have taken this verse to mean that Wu comes before Yo. It is a proclamation that "something" can come from "nothing." This resulted in many debates.

Why did Laotzu emphasize that Yo comes into being from Wu and not the other way around? What is implied by this asymmetry?

In the Oneness state, as shown in Chapter 1, Laotzu proclaims a complete Wu-Yo symmetry with full transmutations. To make our discussions clear, we have to coin a new term, *the Heavenly Yo state*, for the Yo state associated with the Oneness state, taking note of the term *Heavenly Unity* in Chapter 56. The Heavenly Yo state, corresponding to Oneness, is said to be with the Heavenly Te (Chapter 10).

It is clear that Laotzu also considered many other states where we are not in the Heavenly Yo state. We may be in partial synchronization with Tao, but is not in the Oneness state. Each of these states is also a Yo state, where Tao will be effective. Laotzu identified these Yo states by their association with various states of Te, such as Jen, Yi, and Li, and the lost state (in Chapter 38). We may envision each of these Yo states as having partial synchronization with the Wu state.[1]

Therefore, we may see that, in general, Wu cannot come from Yo, but every Yo comes from Wu. Wu can come from Yo probably only in the Oneness state. There is a definite Wu-Yo asymmetry in Tao philosophy. There are many Yo states and only one Wu state.

This observation is similar to what we have arrived in Cosmology, which will be discussed in Section 7. When we describe

---

[1] The Wu state represents the core of Tao. We may say that we cannot fully decode the signals from heaven when we are in a limited Yo state. The signals we can decode are correct, but they are not complete. Only in the Oneness state, the ultimate Yo state can decode all signals.

our physical universe with what each of us observes, each of us will describe the universe differently, but all descriptions should be consistent since there is only one universe.

When we apply this to Tao, each of us may see a different Yo state, but all Yo states are consistent since there is only one Tao or one Wu state. This also clarifies our common interchangeable use of Wu and Tao. We often equate Tao to the Wu state, since there is only one Wu state.[1] In our strict terminology, Tao is Oneness.

3.8   THE YO STATES AND CONFUCIUS

Most of the Confucius teachings are explicit in the Yo domain. With our understanding of Yo-Wu relationship, we should speculate that Laotzu would support what Confucius was doing to help people with Jen, Yi and Li!

Laotzu believed that these teachings are necessary when people are unable to attain the Oneness state. Confucius is a prime example of the Sage, in Laotzu's mind.

3.9   GENERALIZED YO-WU RELATIONSHIP

In the course of our analysis, we also come across another Yo-Wu pair in Chapter 60. We have associated spirit 鬼 with Wu, and god 神 with Yo. We may therefore interpret that chapter in terms of Wu and Yo symmetry.[2]

This is consistent with Guantzu Inner Exercise 內業篇, where he had:

---

[1] Here we should mention that Wang Bi associated Wu with One and Yo with Many. He also equated Tao with Wu. He did not clearly distinguish the concept of One and Oneness. We have clearly distinguished Oneness from One and equated Tao with Oneness.

[2] This interpretation is critical to our understanding of Chapter 60. Lietzu: Gui (Ghost) means to return. Returning to its true place (鬼，歸也，歸其真宅). Return from the explicit state to the implicit state. Shen 神 means manifestation and is translated as god for convenience. We interpreted the essence 精 of Tao in the Guantzu as Chi.

(精) 流於天地之間 *(Chi) Flowing between heaven and earth,*
　　謂之鬼神 *it is called Spirit and God.*

This verse reflects to the process of Chi, in creating the states of Wu and Yo. It is similar to Chapter 1, so we may interpret this verse in the Inner Exercise as: *Tao flows between heaven and earth, and it manifests as Wu and Yo.*

We have adopted this interpretation in our Chapter 60 and avoided introducing s*purious* ghost and *personal* god into Tao philosophy.

The relationship between Wu and Yo states can also be extended to many other linked pairs in Tao philosophy, such as Tao and vessels 器, and substance and functions 體與用. Each pair has a dynamic process similar to Wu-Yo transmutation.

The general properties of Yo-Wu-Oneness triad may exhibit in different levels. We may observe how yin and yang transmutate into each other to form Chi. This is similar to Fractal structure discussed in Section 3.14.

3.10   WU-YO DUALITY

One of the first quantum effects observed was the particle-wave duality of electrons. The properties of an electron are manifested sometimes as waves and sometimes as particles. Depending on the apparatus used to detect the electron, we may see a wave or a particle.

Throughout our effort in analyzing the verses in the Tao Te Ching, we are often reminded of quantum theory in the words of Laotzu. The phenomenon we see in Wu and Yo is similar to this wave-particle duality. We have shown that Wu and Yo are inter-dependent and are superimposed in the Oneness state.

The superposition of Wu and Yo may be more complicated than the particle-wave duality in quantum theory, since particle and wave may be observed independently and Wu and Yo are always transmuting into each other, see Section 3.13.

As in quantum theory, if Wu and Yo are solutions of the Tao field equation, then a linear combination of Wu and Yo is also a solution of the Tao field equation. This may be called the Principle of Superposition[1] in Tao philosophy.

3.11 WU-YO CONNECTION THROUGH DRAGON VEINS

The two states, Yo and Wu, are dualistic and non-dualistic at the same time. Laotzu used a single verse *"Yo and Wu come into being in each other"* to describe this principle. The two states appear as a superimposed state to the Tao universe.

The relationship between yin and yang is commonly shown in the Tai-chi Diagram 太極圖, as shown on the title page of Part II, where there is an eye of yin in yang and an eye of yang in yin. They are the source of transmutation. Yin and yang are connected through these eyes via the *dragon veins* in a higher dimension. Likewise, Wu and Yo are connected in this fashion.[2]

3.12 THE UNCERTAINTY PRINCIPLE

Can we describe an electron as a particle circulating around a nucleus? Physicists found the answer to be "no." A hypothesis was given to resolve this quantum effect. It is known as the Uncertainty Principle of Heisenberg.[3]

There are conjugate physical properties that cannot be determined with arbitrary accuracy. For example, during a very short time, the energy of a particle always has some uncertainty. Momentum and position of a particle can be determined only within certain accuracy at one time.

It is important to point out that the Uncertainty Principle does not say that everything is uncertain. The description of the system, the whole wave function, can be determined with certainty, so any

---

[1] We are using this theory only as a qualitative illustration to the relationship of Wu and Yo. For discussion of general quantum principles, the reader will find abundant resources on the Internet.

[2] In Quantum Cosmology, universes are connected via "wormholes" so they have information of each other through these wormholes.

[3] Werner Heisenberg (1901 –1976) published his theory of quantum mechanics at the age of 23, and was awarded the Nobel Prize in 1932.

combined pairs of energy and time, or momentum and position, may be determined with certainty simultaneously.

The Uncertainty Principle has far-reaching implication in Physics. Time and space are related to fluctuations in energy and momentum, so the distinction of time, space, and matter itself becomes blurred.

When we apply this to Tao, we may say that we cannot exactly identify the Wu and Yo states, since they have constant inter-transmutations. This uncertainty effect is evident when we read the chapters in the Tao Te Ching. If we identify Yo as a conscious state, and Wu as an unconscious state, their constant transmutations will show constant "appearing and disappearing", as described in Chapter 14, 20, and 21. Tao moves in the manner of constant disappearing and appearing.[1]

3.13   QUANTUM ENTANGLEMENT

Quantum entanglement is a quantum mechanical phenomenon in which the quantum states of two or more objects have to be described with reference to each other. This is similar to what we have to do with Wu and Yo in a different domain.

In a simplified form, if we decompose man-heaven interactions via Chi into two components, those contributing to Yo and those contributing to Wu, then the combined solution to describe a Tao state would be an entangled state of Yo and Wu.

In the state of Oneness, there will be terms describing the linked Yo and Wu states. However, Yo and Wu seem to be more complicated than a simple entangled state of two separate states, since Yo and Wu cannot be separated.

---

[1] Cheng Suen-yin 成玄英 in Tang dynasty said, "It is not Yo and not Wu. It is Wu and also Yo. Yo and Wu are indeterminate, so it is called constant disappearing and appearing 「非有非無，而無而有，有無不定，故言惚恍。」

3.14   FRACTAL THEORY OF TAO

Fractal is a geometric shape that can be viewed at any level of magnification and each small portion of the fractal can be viewed as a reduced-scale replica of the whole, see [MA82].

We may apply this theory to Tao philosophy. Laotzu explicitly describes Tao at two levels. The basic triad pattern is described in verses 1 and 2 of Chapter 42. When we look at Oneness, we see the structure of interacting Yo and Wu. In Yo and Wu, we see structure of Chi. Inside Chi, we see the structure of interacting yin and yang. This pattern repeats downwards to infinity.

Without much imagination, we may extend this "Yo-Wu-Oneness" inter-relationship all the way up from Oneness, to super-Oneness, and to holograms of super-Oneness, etc. as discussed in Section 7.5. This structure may also be extended below yin and yang. We may say that the fundamental theory in Tao philosophy is this yin-yang interplay all the way, up and down!

3.15   NOTHINGNESS IN PHYSICS

In classical physics, matter and space are separated, but in modern physics, matter and space are not separable. For detailed discussion on *Nothingness* as the science of empty space, from ancient Greek philosophers to modern sciences, see [GE99].

Readers will recognize some similarity between our modern views on matter and space, and Laotzu's views on Yo and Wu.

It is interesting to note that Genz stated, from his study of nothingness in physics, that "we may take it for granted that the perplexing paradox of being/nonbeing[1] in the Taoist's tale will finally turn out to be the world." [GE99].

---

[1] In this terminology, being is Yo and nonbeing is Wu.

4   The Characteristics of the Wu State 無

Can we really describe the Wu state? Laotzu did it in many of his Chapters. The Wu state is an *unconscious* state of man with respect to his interactions with heaven, so our *conscious* language may not be able to link to the *unconsciousness* effectively.

Wu is the *ultimate return* or concealment of Tao. Wu is not a state of nothingness, but is a state of completeness and harmony.[1] In Tao philosophy, the Wu state is never completely hidden, since there is always a Yo state encoded inside it.

Laotzu has used various keywords to describe the Wu state - it is a state of infancy, Pu 樸 (simplicity), and non-polarity. The Wu state is also often discussed as part of the Oneness state, where Laotzu used *Threads of Tao, Incipient Te, Tzujan (nature), without manifestations, following nature,* and *Heavenly Unity* to describe the Wu state.

Wu is a *positive* state of Tao. This positive nature of Wu must be properly preserved in our interpretation of Tao. For example, Laotzu often used Wu-wei 無爲, Wu-Yue 無欲, and Wu-zhi 無知 as the main attributes of the Wu state. These concepts are of great importance in Tao philosophy. Unfortunately, these terms have been commonly interpreted as *without action*, *without desire*, and *without wisdom*. Such negative interpretations have contributed to gross misunderstandings of Wu, and, more importantly, of Tao.

In the following sections, we want to eradicate such popular negative interpretations and hope to eliminate superficial paradoxes about the Wu state.

4.1   WU AS A STATE

The word Wu 無 is often interpreted as an adjective, so the term Wu-wei 無爲 has been taken to mean *without action*. In our analysis, we concluded that Laotzu has defined Wu as a state and used it as a noun to describe the state.

---

[1]   Wentzu 文子 characterized Wu-sound 無聲 as "five notes resonating 五音鳴 焉," where all sounds are resonating into a perfect harmony.

What is in the Wu state? It is not an empty or nothingness state. Let us use a quantum theoretic model to show the dynamics of the Wu state.

We may illustrate the properties of the Wu state by Figure 3. On the left-hand side, we show vertex (a) as Chi creating a yin-yang pair, and vertex (b) as a yin-yang pair creating Chi (see Chapter 42). These two processes may be combined into the diagram shown on the right-hand side, which is the state of Wu.

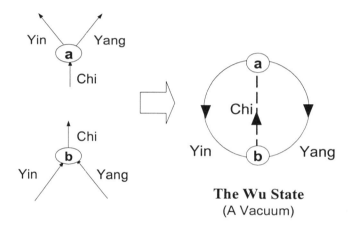

The Wu State
(A Vacuum)

Figure 3   The Wu State - A Vacuum State

This Wu state is called a vacuum state in quantum theory. The vacuum state does not interact with anything outside, so it may appear as "nothingness" to the outside. However, this Tao vacuum is full of internal dynamic Chi. The Wu state represents a state with zero-point internal energy fluctuations. All actions in this Wu state are performed according to the harmonious Chi and are concealed from outside.

4.2   WU-WEI AS WU-ACTION 無爲

It is clear that Wu-wei 無爲 should not be interpreted as without action. Wu-wei is the spontaneous action that maintains harmonious interaction between man and heaven. We have translated Wu-wei

39

literally as Wu-action or as the action according to the Wu state. By acting with Wu, we may maintain our harmony with heaven.

This Wu-action is the action according to Tzujan 自然 (nature). [1] Laotzu also describes this Wu-action as "to act with Wu 無以爲" (Chapter 38). Its relationship to "acting with Yo 有以爲 " is discussed in Section 9.4.

Wentzu also stated that Wu-action is not to act disregarding the nature, but is to *act according to the nature.*[2]

4.3   WU-ZHI AS WU-WISDOM 無知

Some people have argued that Laotzu is anti-wisdom because he promoted ignorance. Laotzu's concept of Wu-zhi 無知 has been interpreted as "without wisdom" or as ignorance.

Such anti-wisdom interpretation has been detrimental to our understanding of Tao. We shall show that this is the most misunderstood concept in Tao. The truth is that Laotzu never showed anything against wisdom or knowledge.[3]

We should interpret Wu-zhi as *the wisdom of the Wu state,* or simply *Wu-wisdom.* This simple re-interpretation gives us a new state of mind to appreciate the positive nature of Tao. Tao becomes much more coherent and pro-wisdom. In fact, we can no longer find any anti-wisdom state in the Tao Te Ching.

For example, we have interpreted the following verse in Chapter 3 as:

3   恒使民   *Always guide the people to*
     無知、無欲也，   *Wu-wisdom and Wu-desire.*

---

[1] This Wu-action is similar to a fundamental law of physics, known as "the *Least Action Principle,*" which states that the natural process must follow the path of least action.

[2] 文子:「無爲者，不先物爲也，順物之性也.」

[3] Many readers may be surprised by this statement. Nevertheless, it is true based on the verses in the Tao Te Ching. Laotzu's view on knowledge is discussed further in Section 5.

With this interpretation, Laotzu actually urges people to seek *positively* the wisdom of the Wu state and the desire for the Wu state. Our interpretation is contrary to the popular statement that Laotzu intended to make people ignorant and without desires.

Successful decoding of Wu-wisdom was a major breakthrough in our reconstruction of a coherent Tao philosophy. Wu-desire is discussed in Section 4.6.

We may apply the same rule to another very difficult verse in Chapter 70. This verse looks very awkward in its sentence structure and has defied a coherent interpretation. But, with our interpretation of Wu-zhi, the verse becomes quite simple as:

70 夫唯無知也，　*Unless by Wu-wisdom,*
　　是以不我知。　*there is no way to understand my principles.*

Our analysis shows that Laotzu plainly urged us to seek his teachings by using the wisdom of the Wu state. [1] There is no mystery in this verse.

4.4　WISDOM AND KNOWLEDGE

Our interpretation of Wu-wisdom comes out of our analysis of the two words, ZHI 知 and zhi 智, used in the Tao Te Ching texts. [2] For convenience, we use capitalized ZHI as wisdom and lower case zhi as knowledge in the following discussion.

These two words are used inter-changeably in many ancient Chinese literature. Laotzu used these words with clear distinction and with consistency in the Tao Te Ching. He used ZHI 知 as wisdom as associated with the Wu state - and zhi 智 as wisdom

---

[1] In Prajna 般若, one may find a similar statement: ' Prajna is Wu-wisdom, so it knows all. 「般若無知，無所不知。」

[2] The 知 and 智 are often used interchangeably in many ancient Chinese classics and their distinctions are often made by the interpreters. Whenever their distinction is observed, 知 is used as wisdom. Logographically, it is interesting to note that 智 is written as "wisdom 知 that lasts over a day 日 only."

associated with the changing world, or the Yo state. So zhi 智 represents *temporary wisdom,* which we identify as knowledge.

Laotzu identifies ZHI (wisdom) with the Wu state and zhi (knowledge) with the Yo state.

4.5   WU-WISDOM AND LEADERSHIP

What is the distinction between ZHI and zhi? Simply put, Laotzu said that the leader should have wisdom of Wu so he can lead. People at least should have enough wisdom of Yo, the knowledge, to be guided to follow Tao.

The wisdom of the Yo state is not sufficient for a ruler to rule, as Laotzu states in Chapter 65:

65 夫民之難治也， 以其智也。	*People are hard to manage, because the ruler relies on his knowledge.*

This interpretation is explicitly stated again in Chapter 75, where Laotzu states,

75 百姓之不治也， 以其上之有以爲也， 是以不治。	*People are hard to manage because the ruler acts with Yo, so he cannot manage.*

This view is also supported by Chapter 57, where Laotzu states, *"When (a leader) acts with Wu-action, people will self-evolve."*

Throughout the Tao Te Ching, we have a consistent interpretation of wisdom of Wu and knowledge of Yo. This interpretation is also consistent with Hsuntzu, who said that, "Knowing within oneself is called wisdom. Knowing corresponding to external things is called knowledge."[1] Lietzu made the same distinction by saying: "Knowledge cannot be wisdom."[2] Wentzu

---

[1] Hsuntzu 荀子 Chapter 22 正名篇:「知之在人者謂之知，知有所合謂之智。」

[2] Lietzu 列子:「智不能知也.」

42

asked, "Seeking the true wisdom, can we attain Wu-wisdom? This is the true wisdom."[1]

Laotzu emphasized that wisdom at the Wu level is the ultimate wisdom that a leader should have in order to manage the people effectively. He also emphasized the importance of knowledge, as the wisdom of the Yo state. We shall discuss Laotzu's views on Yo and knowledge further in Section 5.10.

4.6   WU-YUE AS WU-DESIRE

Wu-Yue 無欲 appears only once in the Tao Te Ching, but it has inspired endless speculations.[2] In our interpretation, Wu-Yue is not without desires, but is the "intrinsic desire to be nurtured by heaven in the Wu-state." We have translated Wu-Yue *literally* as the Wu-desire. It is the proper and positive desire in the Wu-state, without any other desires.

As in the example discussed in the previous section, we interpret Verse 3:7 as "We should always guide the people to Wu-wisdom and Wu-desire."

4.7   OTHER WU-ATTRIBUTES

There are other Wu-attributes that should also be interpreted positively. These terms have not created major mis-interpretations of the Tao Te Ching.

For example, *Wu-shi* 無事, as Wu-efforts or Wu-services, refers to all efforts or services that are proper in the Wu-state. In Verse 63:1 事無事 becomes straightforward as, "to serve with Wu-efforts." Similarly, we have Wu-heart referring to the heart that is in harmony with the Wu-state.

Wu-selfishness 無私 is to keep Self in the Wu-state, and not to have personal concerns. Wu-guide 無執, which appears only once in Chapter 64, means to hold on only to the guidance provided by the Wu-state. Wu-self 無身 is to have self in the Wu state. Wu-

---

[1] Wentzu 文子疏義:「真其實知,能無知乎?是謂實知也.」

[2] Wu-desire appears only once in the Mawangdui version, in Verse 3:7.

management 無治, while never explicitly used by Laotzu, is to rule by Wu, as Wentzu stated: "Wu-management is to not change the nature."[1]

Many of these Wu-attributes appear only a few times in the Tao Te Ching and they can all be associated with the properties of the Wu state.

4.8 YO-WISDOM AND YO-ACTION

It is also interesting to note that, with Wu-Yo symmetry, the attributes associated with the Wu state should also appear in the Yo state. By this extrapolation, we may consider Yo-action 有爲, Yo-desire 有欲, and Yo-wisdom 有知, as proper actions in the Yo state, although Laotzu did not directly use these terms.

4.9 WU AND TAO

Since Wu may be taken to be the anchor of all Yo manifestations of Tao, we may be tempted to treat Wu as Tao itself. To be consistent, Wu is only an integral part of Tao but cannot represent the whole Tao.

It is true that Wu covers the hidden aspect of Tao, but Yo reveals Tao to man. The manifestations of Wu remain hidden from us, so it may appear to be more permanent. Yo appears in a more complicated way to us, but this dynamic manifestation is an integral part of Tao philosophy that cannot be ignored.

Tao should be related to the Oneness state. Laotzu describes the Oneness state as Heavenly Unity 玄同 (Chapter 56), and the associated Te as the Heavenly Te 玄德 (Chapter 10 & 51). The Te associated with the Wu state is the Incipient Te 孔德 (Chapter 21).

---

[1] Wentzu 文子:「無治者，不易自然也.」

5   The Characteristics of the Yo State 有

Although the Yo 有 state has been described in detail in many chapters in the Tao Te Ching, it has not been widely recognized as an intrinsic part of Tao. In some extreme cases, the Yo state is considered to be an undesirable deviation from Tao. In our model, the Yo state is as important as the Wu state.

5.1   YO AS THE WINDOW INTO WU

In the Yo state, man is aware of the interactions with heaven and can sense the reverting power of Tao. Tao acts as a synchronization signal for man to return to the Oneness state. When we are not in the Oneness state, there are many Yo states we could be in; each Yo state corresponds to a particular state of man-heaven interactions and is linked to the Wu state via transmutation.

While we are seeking Tao, the Yo states may be even more important than the Wu state. The Yo states are the doorways to the Oneness state. Without Yo states, there is no redemption for man.[1]

5.2   LAOTZU'S DESCRIPTIONS OF YO

How did Laotzu describe the Yo states? In some cases, Laotzu describes Yo in terms of Te, as the proper laws of interaction. The Yo states are manifestations of Te, the characteristics of which can be traced back to the interaction of Chi. Laotzu also describes Yo as the state that the Sage would try to restore. The Sage's function is to bring a deviated state back to Oneness. The restored states are also the examples of the Yo states.

Therefore, Laotzu describes the Yo states in terms of its relation to Wu, Chi, Te, Oneness, bipolar symmetry, and Sage's actions, etc. Most of Laotzu's discussion of Te is related to the Yo state, with notable exceptions of Heavenly Te and Incipient Te, which are associated with the Oneness state and the Wu state, respectively.

We may recognize properties of the Yo states by observing the following descriptions in the Tao Te Ching:

---

[1]   In this view, the Yo states are viewed as the doorways to the Wu state. This is discussed further in Section 7.

- The transmutation from the Wu state – as initiation of the Yo state,
- Development of the Yo state to its fullness as a Tao system,
- The various characteristics of Te, and
- The actions taken by the Sage.

These are described in the following sections.

5.3   GENERAL PROPERTIES OF YO

Overall, Laotzu describes the Yo states as *Following Tzujan* (Nature) in Chapter 52 and *Greatest Harmony* in Chapter 65. In the Oneness state, Laotzu treats the Yo states as parts of Tzujan and harmony. When the Yo states are not in full harmony with the Oneness state, they may still be considered as part of Tzujan.

5.4   PU, VESSEL, SAGE, AND THE GRAND SYSTEM

There are basic concepts related to the Yo state. Laotzu defines the initiating state of Yo as Pu 樸 (simplicity) and the full state of Yo as the Grand System 大制. The Sage 聖人 will guide people in the Yo state and people will become Vessel 器 when fully synchronized with Tao. They should be treated as keywords in Tao philosophy. The process of forming such a Tao System is described in Chapter 28.

Laotzu defined Pu in Chapter 32 as the very initiation (germinating) state of the Yo state.[1]

32 道恒無，　　*When Tao manifests as true Wu,*
　　名樸。　　　*it is called Pu (Simplicity).*

---

[1]   This very state is the initial transmutation from the true Wu state into the Yo state, as proclaimed in verse 6 of Chapter 1.

The stages to develop a full Tao system are described in Chapter 32. The state of Pu evolves into a Yo state and manifests as an initial Tao system, as described by Laotzu in Chapter 32,

32 始制有名 *When a system is started, it is manifested as Yo.*

This process of Pu development is self-rectifying as described in Chapter 32 and 37.

37 化而欲作，   *When the self-evolution is imminent,*
吾將鎮之以   *we subdue it with*
無名之樸。   *Pu (Simplicity), the un-manifested.*

Once the Pu state is established, the system is further established by diffusing Pu 樸 into all people which makes them the vessels of Tao, under the guidance of the Sage. Finally, the Oneness state is achieved and the final Grand System of Tao is formed. The final stage of forming a Tao system is described by Laotzu in Chapter 28 and 32.

28 樸散則爲器   *Pu diffuses to form (man as) vessels.*
聖人用則爲官長 *The Sage functions to be the leader.*
故大制無割   *Thus, the Grand System is not fragmented.*

Laotzu has described clearly, in Chapter 28, the elements and process in forming this Grand system from the actions of Chi, to the diffusion of Pu (and to vessels) and to the guidance of the Sage.

5.5   TE 德 AND LI 理

What is Te? The meaning of Te has not been extensively explored by scholars.[1] The concept of Te is shown in our model to

---

[1] Translation of Te into a single English word proves to be almost impossible. Te 德 has been translated as Power, Virtue, Character, the Attributes of the Tao, Nature, Efficacy, etc.

be as important as Tao, but Te has not been discussed extensively as a well-defined concept by itself. It may be interesting to explore the reason that this critical term never gained its proper position in Tao philosophy.

Our speculation is that the Te proposed by Laotzu has never been properly understood. In the 12th century, Chinese scholars started to discuss the close relationship between Chi and the newly proposed concept called *Li* 理, which has been translated as the Principles. The school of Li 理學 was thus established and the principle of Tao is essentially discussed in terms of Li 理. We have found that the properties of Li are essentially the same as the properties of Te defined in our field theory. The concept of Te has been substituted by the concept of Li in Chinese philosophy. The proper meaning of Te remains in obscurity.

Laotzu has described several characteristics of Te as the Utmost Te and Lower Te in Chapter 38.[1] He describes the actions with and without Te in Chapter 79. The Utmost Te, Lower Te, the Yo-action, and Wu-action are related, as discussed in Section 9.4.

5.6   A FORMAL DEFINITION OF TE

Laotzu defines Te formally twice in the Tao Te Ching, in Chapter 10 and 51. This formal definition is given as:

10	生而弗有也，	*(Tao) bears without possessing,*
and	爲而弗恃也，	*acts without seeking return, and*
51	長而弗宰也，	*supports without seeking control.*
	是謂玄德。	*It is called the Heavenly Te.*

It is interesting to note that Laotzu repeats this definition and it is not a careless insertion. Chapter 10 describes the Te associated with the Yo state and Chapter 51 describes the Te associated with the Wu state. These two definitions are identical in text, but they have

---

[1]   From the description in Chapter 38, we may deduce that Laotzu recognized Jen 仁 and Yi 義 as part of the Yo state, so people with Jen or Yi can still act with Yo 有以爲。

different meanings because of the context. Laotzu called this ultimate Te in the Oneness state as the *Heavenly Te* 玄德. In the Yo state, this Heavenly Te rules over the actions of man; in the Wu state, it rules over the actions of heaven.

In Chapter 60, Laotzu describes how the Sage and heaven interact via such heavenly Te:

60   故德交歸焉。   *Their Te's interweave and return (to Oneness).*

This ultimate Te is also stated by Wentzu as, "To benefit all without bias and to be in harmony with heaven and earth is called Te." [1] Te is universal in both Yo and Wu states with the transmutation. When the Yo state transmutates into Wu, Te seems to disappear from us. This was described by Antzu (d. 500 B.C.) as: *When Yo disappears, Te returns to Wu.*" [2] Te of the Yo state does not disappear, but only transmutates into the Te of the Wu state. Laotzu called the Te emerging from the Wu state as the Incipient Te 孔德 in Chapter 21.

5.7   CHARACTERISTICS OF TE

The characteristics of Te may be derived from the properties of Chi, which obeys yin-yang symmetry. As in the field theory, the quanta being exchanged determine the characteristics of the interaction. We may observe this relationship in Chapter 28, where Laotzu shows that a *balanced flow of* Chi with yin and yang could trickle like a small creek of Te to return to Oneness:

28   知其雄，守其雌   *Knowing its yang and preserving its yin,*
       恒德不離。   *true Te never departs.*
       復歸於嬰兒。   *All return to Infancy.*

---

[1] Wentzu 文子:「兼利無擇與天地和，此之謂德。」
[2] Antzu 晏子:「微也者，德之歸也。」

This symmetry repeats throughout Chapter 28, with other bipolar properties, emphasizing the need to maintain balances.

5.8   WHAT IS A SAGE?

Our actions should synchronize with the intrinsic properties of the Heavenly Yo state, so that we can return to the Oneness state. Laotzu describes such actions as those taken by the Sage.

What is a Sage? We have found an interesting definition of the Sage proposed by Guantzu in his Inner Exercise Chapter 內業篇 :

(精) 藏於胸中　*(With essence of Tao) concealed in his*
謂之聖人。　　*chest, he is called the Sage.*

From this definition, the Sage is a man in harmony with Chi (the essence of Tao), so the Sage always acts according to the harmonious Chi and the Heavenly Te.

Laotzu associated the Sage only with the Yo states, because the guidance of the Sage is useful only when we need guidance to return to Oneness. The Sage's function to lead is no longer required when the people are in the Oneness state. Chuangtzu has also stated this as follows, *"When Tao prevails under heaven, Sage's work is complete; when there is no Tao, Sages come into being."*[1]

The Sage is a man with the Heavenly Te since he is capable of being in the Oneness state. His Yo actions are directly connected to the Wu state, so he is able to act with Wu. Therefore the Sage is a natural leader for the people, because he is expected to act with Wu. This is consistent with Laotzu's requirement that all leaders should act with Wu, which is explicitly stated in Chapter 75, and discussed further in Section 9.4.

---

[1] Chuangtzu 莊子:「天下有道，聖人成焉；天下無道，聖人生焉。」When Sage's work is complete, he is no longer needed.

5.9   WHAT WOULD THE SAGE DO?

One way to find out what actions are proper in a situation is to ask what the Sage would do in that situation. His action would reflect the proper Yo action to be in harmony with the way of Tao.

We have many such examples of Sage's actions in the Tao Te Ching that describe the Yo state. As one example, we have, from Chapter 22:

22 是以聖人執一，	*Therefore, the Sage abides with Oneness as*
以爲天下牧。	*the guide for all under heaven.*
不自見故明；	*By not self-showing, he is illuminating.*
不自是故彰；	*By not self-asserting, he is conspicuous.*
不自伐故有功；	*By not self-boasting, he receives praise.*
弗矜故能長。	*By not self-glorifying, he sustains.*

All examples given by Laotzu are very specific and can provide clear guidance for man to follow.

5.10   YO AND KNOWLEDGE

Did Laotzu value knowledge? This is another area where we greatly misunderstood his teachings. We often think that Laotzu is anti-wisdom and knowledge.

We are all perplexed when it appears that Laotzu declares we should end Sageness and abandon knowledge:

19 絕聖棄智，	*End Sageness and abandon knowledge,*
民利百倍；	*and people will benefit a hundredfold.*

There is actually no paradox in this verse. If we understand Laotzu's basic requirement for a leader is to be able to act according to Wu, we will not be puzzled by what Laotzu meant in this verse.

Chapter 19 describes the actions in the Wu state or the Oneness state, so knowledge and Sageness are no longer useful. Acting with Yo (i.e., acting with knowledge) and Sageness are useful only in the

Yo state. We did not see any of Laotzu's statements as anti-knowledge for common people in the Yo state.

After all, he has shared his wisdom/knowledge with common people through his Chapters. Also, as stated in Chapter 71, he would not dislike anything and that should include the knowledge that people have.

5.11   YO, TE, AND TAO

The Yo state represents what we can perceive in Tao. In the Oneness state, the Yo state that reflects the Wu state is a special Yo state. When we are in the Oneness state, Wu and Yo become one and will show their constant process of transmutations.

When we are not in the Oneness state, we will perceive our interactions with heaven in many ways. Each way represents a Yo state and there are many such Yo states. However, all Yo states are the results of the universal laws of Te, as discussed in Section 3.4.

The relationship between the Yo states and Wu will be discussed again in terms of the holographic principle in Section 7.

6 Debates on Yo and Wu 有無之爭

Many schools of Chinese philosophy resulted from intensive debates on the concepts of Wu and Yo during and after the Wei and Jin dynasties 魏晉時代 (269-534). It is not clear how and why Wu and Yo became the focus of debate. Perhaps, they simply did not recognize the relationships between Yo and Wu as stated by Laotzu.

The historical evolution of Wu and Yo debates has been discussed in detail by Xu Kangsheng and Ke Jong Jin [Xu93, Ge01].

6.1 THE PRO-WU AND PRO-YO GROUPS

Both groups perceived the state of Wu as a more fundamental state, because the Yo state appeared to be less certain. For this reason, the philosophers were split into two groups.

A Pro-Wu group 貴無派 emphasized Wu as the essence of Tao, and thus minimized the importance of Yo, to the extent that Yo was treated as deviations from Tao. This group is represented by Ho An 何晏 (193-249) and Wang Bi 王弼 (226-249).

The other group, the Pro-Yo group 崇有派, emphasized the importance of Yo as the way to reach harmony with heaven. This group, represented by Shiang Shiu 向秀 (227-272) and Kuo Shiang 郭象 (252-312), considered Wu too mysterious to provide guidance. The Pro-Yo group claimed that the explicit teachings (as Yo) represented the ultimate the Tzujan 名教即是自然.

The debate continued through the South-North Dynasty 南北朝 and the Tang Dynasty, when Tao started to merge with the newly introduced Buddhism.

6.2 A UNIFIED VIEW

During the Tang dynasty, Taoist Cheng Shuen-ying 成玄英 (630-660) and Buddhist Liu Chong-yuen 柳宗元 (773-819) each proposed a unified view of Wu and Yo. This unified concept merged with Tao, Buddhism, and Confucianism. Liu proposed a Theory of Original Chi 元氣論. Chu-hsi 朱熹 (1130-1200) used Principles 理 to explain Wu and Yo.

Another group led by Chang Dai 張戴 (1020-1077) established the School of Chi 氣學派 and proposed that Ultimate Virtuality 太虛 is Chi. He recognized that if the ultimate emptiness is full of Chi, then Yo and Wu should become One and not Two.[1]

In the Ming Dynasty, Wang Fuzhi 王夫之 (1619-1692) further consolidated Chinese philosophy of Wu and Yo with Chi. He classified whatever we could feel as Yo and whatever we could not feel as Wu. Wang Fuzhi viewed Yo-Wu as a dynamic process and recognized that everything has both Yo and Wu in a mutual transmutation.[2]

6.3   LAOTZU'S UNIFIED THEORY

In Laotzu's formalism, Wu and Yo appear with equal importance. Tao is clearly Pro-Wu *and* Pro-Yo. Both Pro-Wu and Pro-Yo camps are correct to emphasize Wu and Yo respectively. The deviation from Tao philosophy was their great bias against each other. It may be useful to re-visit their propositions and to consolidate a coherent unified philosophy based on their Pro-Wu and Pro-Yo attributes.

Our model provides a foundation to ease the historical debates on Wu and Yo, based on the words of Laotzu.

6.4   A PHILOSOPHICAL DISCONTINUITY

It is not clear how and why Laotzu's original coherent philosophy started to disintegrate right after his death. The Yo-Wu split seems to have been immediate.

We may speculate that Laotzu did not formally pass his ideas through a chain of close disciples, who could have understood Laotzu's original philosophy in a coherent manner. This is consistent with the legend that he wrote the Tao Te Ching on short notice. In that case, he would not have had time to personally teach based on that book. Another possibility could be that the

---

[1]   Chang Dai 張戴:「太虛即氣」 and 「知空虛即氣，則有無、隱顯、神化、性命通一無二。

[2]   Wang Fuzhi 王夫之:「相承而無不可通。」

philosophers' biased views could have been fueled by the desires of the royal courts at the time.[1]

The Pro-Yo and Pro-Wu group could also have been the natural emergence of the dualistic thinking in Chinese philosophy.

6.5   DEBATES ON SOMETHING AND NOTHING

The Yo-Wu debate is not without its parallel in Physics. The natural scientists have long struggled with the question of "something and nothing" in our world.

With the development of quantum theory and relativity, the distinction between "something (matter)" and "nothing (space)" becomes blurred. We have become more willing to accept a unified view of matter, time, and space into a theory of Oneness.

This is exactly the frame of reference that Tao philosophers can use to decode the Tao Te Ching. In the next Section, we shall show that the dynamics of Tao may be described in a way similar to the way we describe the universe.[2]

---

[1] It is interesting to speculate the impact on Tao Te Ching by the desire of First Emperor of Chin (秦始皇) to unify Chinese thinking and by the fact that Confucianism was made a state official doctrine in the Han Dynasty. Was it possible that the original teachings became extinct because of royal courts?

[2] We have not attempted to "explain" any Tao concept with Quantum Cosmology. We simply state that the way Laotzu describes Tao philosophy is similar to the way our physicists describe the observation of our physical universe. Quantum Cosmology provides a platform for us to sort out the relationships between many Tao concepts and dynamics.

7 Tao and the Holographic Principle

Venturing to the farthest frontier of our scientific research brings obvious risks, but the similarity is too interesting to ignore.

Recently, scientists have arrived at a critical point in their dreams of unifying all physical theories into a single unified theory. For the last 50 years, extensive research efforts in particle physics, black hole thermodynamics, quantum gravity and string theory finally led towards a unified theory of the universe. For our purposes, we shall consider a conclusion from the Quantum Cosmology that the universe may be represented as holograms. This holographic principle is discussed in details in [HA01] and [SM01].

Our analogy should not be taken literally, because we have not figured out why these two concepts, Tao and the holographic principle, should be so similar to each other. Is it by accident or by design? Or it could be a hologram in our mind.[1]

7.1 INFORMATION IN QUANTUM COSMOLOGY

After quantum theory and general relativity are applied to cosmology, we have a unified theory called Quantum Cosmology that applies to microscopic and macroscopic universes. This field has attracted the best minds in science for the last few decades. There are many theories, such as the superstring theories, quantum gravity, black hole thermodynamics, etc. There are still many changing developments in this field.[2]

In 1974, S. Hawking showed, with a simple formula, that the black hole entropy is equal to the area of the horizon of the black hole. Entropy of a system is a measure of total information in a system. This means *"there is one bit of information about the*

---

[1] A hologram is a two-dimensional image of a three-dimensional object. When viewed from different angles, the object is also seen from different angles. We have depicted a holographic picture of our Tao universe on the cover of this book.

[2] The most recent change about black hole theory is what S. Hawking announced in July, 2004 that, "If you jump into a black hole, your mass energy will be returned to our Universe, but in a mangled form, which contains information about what you were like, but in an unrecognizable state."

internal state of the black hole for each fundamental unit of area of the horizon." and *"information about what happens in a region of space-time can be encoded on its boundary"* [HA01].

The amount of information that can be displayed on a surface is limited, since the surface of time and space has atomic structure, so they cannot be infinitely small – similar to the finite grid of a TV screen. This finding has been associated with the holographic principle[1] [SM01]. We have found their conclusions may be applied to what has been described by Laotzu about Yo and Wu.

7.2   THE HOLOGRAPHIC PRINCIPLE

We may extrapolate the holographic principle to formulate a new representation of Yo and Wu in Tao philosophy. The analogy may be illustrated in Figure 4.

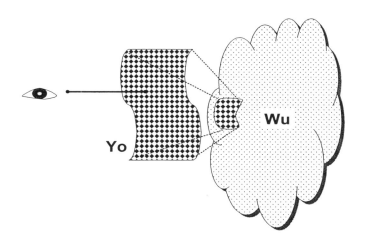

Figure 4   Tao and the holographic principle

The state of Wu is inside the Tao universe and what we can observe is on the surface. This figure shows what we can see on the screen display as the Yo state. This Yo surface of the Tao universe is connected to Wu in the unseen volume. We may retrieve information about Tao by asking questions. The answers are

---

[1]   Proposed by Gerard 't Hooft (1946-) in 1993, who shared a Nobel Prize with Martinia Veltman in 1999.

displayed on the screen. The screen is of limited area, so the information that we can observe at each time is limited. When we ask different sets of questions, we may have different sets of answers, so there are many possible screen displays, and each depends on the questions we ask. At any time, we can only see a limited amount of information. Obviously the scope of Yo is limited, but Wu may be limitless. The transmutation process is hidden from our view.

As we increase the display size and accept more answers from Wu, we may reach the Oneness state, where we may directly observe the dynamic transmutations of Yo and Wu and see Tao directly by staying inside the Tao universe.

Most of the time, we are not in the Oneness state, so each of us will see a different Yo state, whose scope depends on the state of the observer. We may say that each one of us will see a holographic view of Wu, as shown in Figure 5.

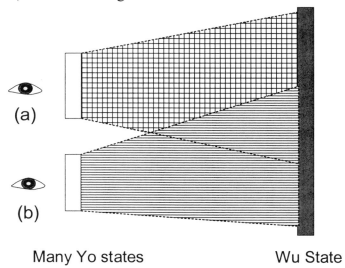

(a)

(b)

Many Yo states   Wu State

Figure 5 Holographic Yo States

Observers (a) and (b) will see two different Yo states, both of which are holograms of the Wu state.

We may associate our Yo states with our concerns/questions at hand and our capacity to perceive Tao. The concerns are relayed to

58

the Wu state and the responses are displayed in our minds (the screens). Every query in the Yo state has an answer from the Wu state, but the scopes of Yo are limited while Wu remains limitless.

This holographic principle provides a convenient way to delineate the relationships between Yo and Wu, as Laotzu states in the Tao Te Ching.

7.3 PRO-YO (STRONG) AND PRO-WU (WEAK) GROUPS

The holographic theory is still under development in theoretical physics.[1] There are, however, strong similarities that unavoidably remind us of the development of the Pro-Yo and Pro-Wu groups after Laotzu proposed his Yo-Wu model.

Since all observable information is only on the screen, one group of scientists suggests that we should model the screen only. This is called the *Screen Theory* or the Strong Holographic Principle [SM01]. In Tao philosophy, this group is known as the Pro-Yo group 崇有派. Kuo Shiang 郭象 (252-312) was one of those who emphasized the importance of Yo as a way to reach harmony with heaven. From this respect, Confucius was a genuine screen theorist.

There is another group of physicists who believe that we cannot express the world in terms of what we can see on the screen, and we have to make direct references to the processes that are happening in the universe. This is called the Weak Holographic Principle. This group of physicists attempts to describe the "information exchanged among physical processes, " instead of the screen and the objects (in Wu).

In Tao philosophy, the Pro-Wu group 貴無派 wanted to ignore the screen itself and try to interact directly with the Wu state[2]. Wang Bi 王弼 (226-249) was one of those who emphasized that Wu is the essence of Tao, and Yo should be minimized.

---

[1] Our discussion of theoretical physics is not complete and should not be taken literally. Our readers should consult our references for a more complete view of the theory [SM01].

[2] Historically, the Wu state has not been clearly distinguished from the Oneness state. For example, Wang Bi considered Wu as One. The Weak Holographic Principle may also be viewed as a Pro-Oneness group.

7.4   THE ONENESS STATE (THE FUNDAMENTAL THEORY)

The Screen Theory seems to allow us to observe the universe from the outside. We may look at Tao from the Yo states, or we may enter the Oneness state, where we are inside the Tao universe with heaven and earth.

What happens when we are inside the universe? We have access to the complete display of information, which is still limited by the area of the surface. We see a complete set of holograms of the universe. These holograms are networked, through internal processes, like transmutations! As Smolin describes the universe in his book [SM01], "The world must be a network of holograms, each of which contains *coded within it* information about the relationships between the others;" and "the world is a network of relationships."

We already know that the Yo state contains *coded within it* information about the Wu state, and vice versa! In the Oneness state, we may consider this Yo-Wu transmutation as a hologram of the Oneness state. In the ultimate Tao universe, it is probably like a networked holograms of many Oneness states.

The results of cosmology research will certainly help us interpret the Oneness state and the ultimate Tao universe.

7.5   THE HOLOGRAMS AS TZUJAN 自然

The ultimate state of Tao, then, is more than just the natural duality state of Oneness. It represents the natural state of all beings and is described by Laotzu as the Tzujan 自然.[1] This ultimate state of nature is a full set of holograms of Oneness, in which man will always feel the interactions with heaven. Man may feel the power of Tao in the Yo state, and sometimes in the Wu state.

With constant transmutations of yin and yang, we feel the reverting power of Chi; with constant transmutations of Wu and Yo, we feel the reverting power of the Oneness state.

---

[1]   The state of Tzujan is a state of total naturalness. We may think of it in a similar way that we describe the Higgs field. The universe becomes not totally symmetrical and begins to show domination of a mysterious field. This is called symmetry breaking in the quantum field theory of particles, and is a natural effect of the Higgs field.

With constant transmutation of the Oneness states, we may consider a Oneness state as a hologram for the Oneness state at the next higher level. We may consider yin-yang as a hologram of Chi, and Yo-Wu as a hologram of Oneness. This concept may be extrapolated to the ultimate state of Tzujan of Laotzu.[1]

The Oneness state is always dynamic.[2]

7.6   THE MYSTERY

So far we might have been amazed by such astonishing scientific descriptions of our universe that we can apply directly to our understanding of Tao, without much speculation. Why do our interpretations of Tao come so close to a theory that involves the most complicated and rigorous mathematics and physics formulations in history?

I do not know why. But the evidence is clear that Laotzu has described an inner universe in a way that is consistent with our understanding of the physical universe so far. It is also safe to assume that this aspect of Tao philosophy has not influenced previous developments in physics - as it is just now being brought to light.

The similarities between Tao and the holographic principle seem to be more than just accidental. This will remain as a mystery. The intricate transmutation relationships of Yo and Wu have been described by Laotzu in the Tao Te Ching. They have been encoded in the poetic form. The holographic principle helped bring the relationships between multiple Yo states and the singular Wu state to an elegant representation.

---

[1]   The yin-yang-Chi and Wu-Yo-Oneness triads form the basic relationship in Tao. We may extend this triad relationship upward or downward indefinitely. We may say that the Tao principle based on yin-yang all the way down and Wu-Yo all the way up.

[2]   We may also see this concept in the I-Ching 易經. The character "I or Yi 易" is often considered to mean "changes." Such an explanation neglects the "unchanging 不易" nature of Yi. In 易緯乾鑿度, we have "The so-called Yi is changing and it is unchanging 所謂易也，變易也，不易也。 " The Greatest Yi 太易 is synonymous with Greatest Oneness 太一。

The description of the Oneness state in terms of networked holograms echoes so well what Laotzu said in Chapter 21,

21	道之物，	*Tao, when perceptible, is like*
	唯恍唯惚。	*fleeting appearances and disappearances.*
	惚呵恍呵，	*Disappearing and then appearing,*
	中有象呵。	*there is an image within.*
	恍呵惚呵，	*Appearing and then disappearing,*
	中有物呵。	*there is substance within.*
	窈呵冥呵，	*Hidden and concealed,*
	其中有情呵。	*there is essence within.*

The discovery of this unexpected convergence adds to all the mysteries we have in our inner minds and the universe.

7.7   A STATE OF COSMOLOGICAL ONENESS

This discovery may be too near the edge of believability, yet quantum cosmology and Tao philosophy do share quite similar mysteries. Moreover, there is no apparent reason why our inner universe should not be similar to the physical universe.

Discovering a common fundamental view of the cosmos and ourselves has been our goal in pursuing Tao philosophy. This may bring a peaceful resolution to any concern that the two might be in conflict.

8   Tao Philosophy and Religions

It is clear that we have not interpreted the Tao Te Ching as a religious text. However, many messages may be construed to have significant religious importance. Tao philosophy was probably not intended by Laotzu to be a religion. Tao was in fact a brave breakaway from the traditional religions at that time.

There is no deity to reward the good and to punish the evil. The ruler has no divine power. Tao seems to be beyond good and evil. There is no external salvation plan for an eternal life. There is no external evil power to cause sin and sufferings. Man is born without a mission to glorify or to change the world, but to live with the world. There is no proclaimed end of the world. There is no discussion of heaven and no hell to receive us after death.

8.1   FOUNDATION OF RELIGIONS

There are clear gaps between Tao and religions, but they may be easily filled by the interpreter to support his or her religion. Tao assures us that there is always a path to salvation. There is always a power beyond description that will guide us back to peace. We have to be able to cultivate our love and trust, and to follow a path of self-salvation, by returning to the Tzujan state with whatever is chosen as our redeemer.

Tao, as we can see, does not intend to be a forceful traditional religion, but there are clear guiding principles that may be developed into a religious philosophy and used as doctrines. Tao has been practiced successfully by many as a philosophical religion. Its basic teachings have also entered into the religions of Daoism, Zen, and Chinese Buddhism.

To be consistent with what he preached, Laotzu would not have any objection to have his teachings practiced as part of a religion. Understanding Tao philosophy will certainly help all religious persons appreciate their religions. Many of us have already enjoyed Tao as a way to have peace with nature, with or without the support of a traditional religion.

8.2   THE ULTIMATE ONENESS

Within the Oneness state, Wu and Yo lose their identities and merge into a higher state. There may be many holographic Oneness states. These states are like fractal units for a larger state. We may reach an ultimate state, which may be thought of as a collection of networked Oneness states. This ultimate state consists of holograms that can be developed into many philosophies and religions.

We can all merge into an Ultimate Oneness state, from which we may diverge again, as Laotzu states in Chapter 28:

28 恒德不忒，　　*When True Te never loses its ability,*
　　復歸於無極。　*all return to the Ultimate Oneness.*
　　樸散則爲器。　*Pu can then disperse to form different vessels.*

8.3   THE ANTHROPIC PRINCIPLE

As described by Laotzu, man could be equal with heaven and earth. Tao is not an authority to be feared or worshiped. Man has a special place in the universe and is capable of seeking guidance from Tao and unifying with heaven and earth.

Therefore, Tao philosophy may be a foundation for anyone who personally feels close to an omnipresent power in a religious world.

9   Remarks on Interpretations

We have identified the internal dynamics of Tao and they may be applied to the interpretation of the Tao Te Ching.

The Tao philosophy is shown to be free of the usual negative speculations. Tao appears to be very dynamic and coherent. We have been able to resolve many ambiguities and contradictions that have plagued our views of Tao. Not only can we coherently interpret these troubling verses, we may also discover new and more enlightening interpretations of many less obvious verses. A few examples will be discussed here.

9.1   THE STATE OF THE VERSES

When we analyze each chapter, it is important to identify the context of each chapter in terms of the state it is describing, so we can orient our minds with the proper frame of reference in order to recognize the message correctly. With improper orientation, we will encounter paradoxes and contradictions.

Each chapter is often related to a Tao state: Wu, Yo, or Oneness and the meaning of a verse depends on the state of the chapter. Our interpretation will be paradoxical and contradictory if we interpret a verse in the wrong state.

Our first example is the well-known paradox of Chapter 56,

56 知者弗言，   *Whoever has wisdom no longer teaches.*
　　言者弗知。   *Whoever (still) teaches shows no wisdom.*

This verse has plagued our thinking for a long time, when it is interpreted as: "Those who have wisdom do not speak, and those who speak do not have wisdom." This verse is certainly paradoxical when we want to be taught about Tao.

To resolve this paradox, we need to recall that teaching is done only in the Yo state and this chapter is describing the Wu state or the Oneness state. In the Wu state, there is no need to teach anymore. If we try to teach in the Wu state, it simply shows our ignorance of the way of Tao.

The keyword to recognize this chapter as related to the Wu state is Laotzu's use of Heavenly Unity 玄同 in the chapter to describe the ultimate unity with Tao. We recognize this state as the utmost harmonious state, so we call it *heavenly*, instead of just mysterious.

The following puzzling verse may be resolved in the same way. Laotzu states in Chapter 19 that

> 19 絕聖棄智 *Excel in (true) Sageness and go beyond knowledge,*
> 民利百倍 *then people will benefit a hundredfold.*

This chapter again describes the Wu state, so there is no need for the Sage to teach and wisdom should prevail. The Sage and knowledge are useful only in the Yo state, as we have noted in Section 5.8.

In the Wu state, we seek Wu-wisdom and Heavenly Unity with Tao. In the Yo state, the Sage remains important.

There are other similar cases in the Tao Te Ching where the state is important and must be considered in order to get a coherent interpretation.

9.2 REPEATED TEXTS

Our second example is the interpretation of repeated texts in the chapters.[1] There are a few groups of verses repeated verbatim in more than one chapter. These have been puzzling throughout history.

We shall show why these verses are repeated and how we can interpret them coherently. For example, Laotzu repeated the following verse in Chapter 52 and in Chapter 56. In Chapter 52, we interpret it as:

> 52 塞其兌， *Plug our flows of desire, and*
> 閉其門 *shut our doors to gratifications.*

---

[1] There are many speculations about the repeated texts in the TTC. Some considered it careless insertions by commentators, and some used it as evidence that the TTC had multiple authors. Many attempted to eliminate the repetitions.

And, in Chapter 56, we interpret the same verse as:

56 塞其兌，　　*Flows of desire are plugged.*
　　閉其門，　　*Doors to gratification are shut.*

Here we have recognized that Chapter 52 describes proper conduct in the Yo state, while Chapter 56 describes that, in the Wu state, the flows are already plugged and the doors are shut.

This example again shows the importance of the state-context of the verse. The two identical Chinese texts were used to describe the same actions in two different states. Their repetition is justified.

As we have discussed in Section 5.6, the definition of Heavenly Te 玄德 is also repeated in Chapter 10 and Chapter 51.

10　　生而弗有也，　　*(Tao) bears without possessing,*
and　　為而弗恃也，　　*acts without seeking return, and*
51　　長而弗宰也，　　*supports without seeking control.*
　　是謂玄德。　　*It is called the Heavenly Te.*

Heavenly Te in Chapter 10 refers to the actions of man in the Yo state and in Chapter 51 refers to the actions of heaven in the Yo state. Therefore, there is a distinction.

Another interesting repetition of Chinese texts is within Chapter 34, 萬物歸焉而弗為主, which we have coherently interpreted as described in the verse-by-verse translation.

We also take note of the repetition of the phrase 恒無 in Chapter 1, 32, 34, and 37.

9.3　Wu-Yo Pair

The complementary pairs of Yo and Wu are commonly used to describe the intrinsic symmetry in Tao. This pair may be yin and yang, high and low, hard and easy, etc. In a few of the chapters, this symmetry becomes important. When such symmetry is not observed, the verses become ambiguous and hard to interpret.

For example, the wording of Wu and Yo in Chapter 11 has led to many awkward interpretations. There is always an extra Chinese character Yo hanging in the middle of the verse that is hard to accommodate in the interpretation.[1] To preserve the Wu-Yo symmetry, we have the following new interpretation:

11　卅輻共一轂，　　*With thirty spokes connected to the hub,*
　　當其無有，　　　*it is its Wu and Yo that*
　　車之用也。　　　*make a wagon functional.*

With this new interpretation, the symmetry of Wu and Yo is fully displayed and the chapter conveys a very coherent picture of the functions of Wu and Yo in Tao philosophy.

There are other symmetry pairs in the Tao Te Ching that have not been widely recognized. For example, Chapter 60 has been difficult to interpret, because we do not recognize the Wu-Yo symmetry.

Part of the confusion is due to the fact that Laotzu associated spirit 鬼 with the Wu state and god 神 with the Yo state.[2] With this observation, we arrived at the following interpretation:

60　以道蒞天下，　*When Tao presides under heaven,*
　　其鬼不神。　　　*its spirit (Wu) remains un-manifested.*

We have interpreted spirit as Wu and god as manifestation. With this symmetry, Chapter 60 can be interpreted with much greater coherence. This also avoids the notion of ghost and god in the basic Tao philosophy. Laotzu further stated that the Te of the two (Wu and Yo) would not interfere with each other and will return to the Oneness state.

---

[1]　It is commonly interpreted as "It is its Wu that makes a wagon useful." This punctuation ignores the word Yo in the verse.

[2]　These interpretations, ghost as Wu and god as manifestation, are actually commonly done in ancient Chinese philosophy.

9.4   ACT-WITH-YO 有以爲 AND ACT-WITH-WU 無以爲

Now we come to a very interesting discovery of the relationship among Wu, Yo, and Te. This relationship turns out to be very fundamental in building a coherent Tao philosophy. When we understand the following examples, we will appreciate fully the importance of the Yo state in Tao philosophy.

Our analysis shows that the Yo state is not a deviation from Tao. The following verse is a good illustration of how a Yo state is envisioned by Laotzu. Laotzu said in Chapter 38,

38 上德無爲 而無以爲也；	*When a man of utmost Te acts with Wu-action,* *he acts according to Wu.*
上義爲之 而有以爲也。	*When a man of utmost righteousness acts,* *he acts according to Yo.*

The concept of acting with Wu 無以爲 has been understood as Wu-action. The discovery is in the meaning of "to act with Yo 有以爲。" Often this phrase *"to act with Yo"* has been interpreted as being unable to act (properly or with Wu) in Tao, and thus carrying a notion of being a deviation from Tao.

We have thus recovered an important meaning of *acting with Yo* as "to rely on the manifestations of Tao (as Yo) to act properly." From this, we may see the main view of Laotzu is that a leader should be able to perform Wu-actions, i.e., to act with Wu 無以爲。 The common people may not be able to act with Wu-actions so they should follow the guidance of the Yo state, i.e., to act with Yo.

This interpretation is also consistent with the modern Chinese usage, where the phrase "to act with Yo 有爲" has been used as an honored appraisal for a person who has performed with positive contributions and is useful in the society. This view is echoed in Chuangtzu Chapter 13, where he stated that "the leader should act with Wu in order to manage the world and the people should act with Yo in order to be useful to heaven and earth." [1]

---

[1] Chuangtzu Chapter 13: 「上必無爲而用天下，下必有爲爲天下用。」

In case a leader loses his ability to act with Wu, his management cannot be in good order, as Laotzu said in Chapter 75:

75 百姓之不治也，
以其上之有以爲也，
是以不治。

People become hard to manage because the leader acts with Yo, so he cannot manage.

This view is again emphasized in Chapter 48, where Laotzu said,

48 取天下也，
恒無事。
及其有事也，
不足以取天下。

Managing the world should always be with Wu-efforts. If it demands (Yo) efforts, one will not be capable of managing the world.

This interpretation is also echoed in Wentzu, who stated, "Those who rely on Tao to lead are not to act with Yo, but to act with Wu."[1] This shows that acting-with-Yo 有以爲 is an important step for man who seeks a return to the Oneness state, but not for a leader who should already be close to the Oneness state.

9.5   OTHER CONVENTIONS USED IN TRANSLATION

The following discussions concern the usage of individual Chinese characters and are of particular interest only to those who are familiar with the Chinese characters. Many of these characters are clarified here and are reflected in our verse-to-verse translation.

For example, interpretation of Verse 5.1 as "Heaven and earth are ruthless 天地不仁 " would be inconsistent with the convention that "the greatest benevolence shows no benevolence."[2]

We observe the conventional distinction among 天 heaven, 天下 under heaven, and 天地 heaven and earth. Heaven[1] is Tao, and

---

[1] Wen-tzu 文子:「君道者，非所以有爲也，所以無爲也。」
[2] Chuangtzu Chapter 2: Greatest Benevolence shows no benevolence 大仁不仁.

heaven and earth is Tzujan 自然. Sometimes, we translate Tzujan as nature, which means the intrinsic characteristics of Tao. Under heaven is also taken to mean the world or a country. We have associated the word 玄 with heaven instead of mystery.

We recognize that some words are used interchangeably: such as *Te* 德 and *attain* 得, *see* 見 and *display* 現. The word *fei* 非 does not always mean negation. The words 絕 and 棄 may be associated with some uncommon connotations. The word 絕 is used in the sense of *absolute* 絕對 and *utmost* 絕世 in Chapter 19, although a casual translation as terminate and abandon respectively will also render a consistent interpretation.

The concept of being full 盈 or complete 成 is subtle. When a vessel is full, it can no longer serve as a useful vessel. Laotzu emphasizes *not to be complete* 免成 (41:09) or 不成 (15:14). In Chapter 45, he stated that the *Greatest Completion* 大成 is not to complete, since, when the function of the Sage is complete, he is no longer useful.

The word 貝 is cowry or shell that was used as money in ancient China. The root word 貝 appears as part of 賢 and 貨 in Chapter 3 and in Chapter 77. We interpret 賢 as the wealth and 貨 as the goods, as cited in [CH00]. This also helps us interpret the word 資 in Chapter 27 as resources.

We have identified Yo 有 as an explicit manifestation 名 of Tao, so 名有 in Chapter 34 is then manifestation of Yo. The term 弗有 in Chapter 10, 51, and 77 means without manifestation or without showing the efforts.

A few particular logographic analyses add coherence to the interpretations. We interpret 恍 as "appearing" because it contains "light 光", and 惚 as "disappearing" because it contains "without mind, sudden 忽". We recognize 智 as temporary wisdom 知 lasting over a day 日. Mind and heart are interchangeably used for *Shin* 心.

---

[1]   Heaven is Tian, which represents *Tao* in the Tao Te Ching. . We have to note that *heaven* here is very different from the Christianity Heaven, which is translated as 天堂 in Chinese that means the *Hall in Heaven*.

71

The word "king 王" has been used by Laotzu in an interesting way. As seen in Chapter 16 and 66, 王 does not assume its most common meaning of an emperor or a king, but is closely associated with the word "homing towards 往." We have also followed a common numbering convention by taking "Ten *you* three" to be thirteen, since *Yo* 有 and *you* 又 were interchangeably used in ancient works to mean "plus." Man is used in the translation of Jen 人, which has no gender differentiation.

In order to make the translation easier to read, we do not translate a Chinese word into a fixed English word. For example, *Heng* 恆 is translated as constant, often, and true. *Min* 明 is translated into insight, enlightenment, observation, and illumination. Mother 母 is also translated as the source or the principle, and son 子 is translated as manifestation. We take this liberty only when they make our interpretations simpler.

10   Laotzu's Philosophy in a New Light

We started this project with the single goal of translating the Tao Te Ching accurately into English. We have gone through many unexpected and very fruitful exercises that guided us to this stage. The results are far more than what we could have imagined before.

We have achieved a major milestone in understanding the Tao philosophy, but our study in this direction is only a first step. We have yet to fully explore what impact this new understanding of Tao philosophy might have upon historical interpretations of the Tao Te Ching itself and the development of Chinese philosophy in general.

10.1   PARADOXES

Without elaborate speculation, we have resolved most, if not all, of the paradoxes and mysteries that have been with us since the Tao Te Ching was created 2500 years ago. Our efforts - quite unexpectedly - have established a modern framework for future studies of Tao philosophy, and the framework parallels ongoing scientific endeavors. The mysteries of Tao have finally been connected to the mysteries of the physical universe.

10.2   A MODERN TAO PHILOSOPHY?

We have not created a modern Tao philosophy; what we have presented is simply a restoration of the original Tao philosophy as described by Laotzu. Great care was taken not to bring anything new to his words. The Tao Te Ching was treated with utmost respect and not altered in any way.

What was changed, however, was the frame of reference used. It was our *minds* that drastically changed in order to accept and fully realize what Laotzu said. The change is in the same manner that we changed to accept quantum theory, relativity and quantum gravity. We changed to recognize and accept the model of Tao that was *originally presented* by Laotzu.

10.3   A TALE OF TWO UNIVERSES

This is the first time the dynamics in Tao philosophy have been clearly demonstrated, and can now be linked to observations in our vast universe. The poetic encoding of Tao dynamics in the Tao Te Ching is clear but not obvious. Our understanding of the laws of nature (physics) has now paved a way for us to describe the full dynamics of Tao in a similar framework. It is a surprise, but our inner universe indeed reflects the outer universe in a consistent way.[1]

This is an indication of a great convergence of the two universes. Such unification may serve as the base for our next leap onto new plateaus.[2]

10.4   NEW MINDS, OPEN DOORS

The way we study Tao will take a new turn into an unknown dimension. Now Tao may be comprehended as a coherent and consistent philosophy. With this new foundation, we may extrapolate our new understanding of Tao towards other human endeavors, perhaps, with a similar impact that other scientific philosophies have had on our daily lives.

It will take a while before we fully realize what we have found. As for now, we should take some time to ponder on the amazing correlation and coherency that has come to light. With such a proper orientation of our minds, we may enjoy a coherent presentation of the Tao Te Ching. The translation presented in Part II will reflect that coherency, and may be used as a new base for unlimited personal speculations.

A new door has opened to all.

---

[1] This is also a fundamental Buddhist view that our inner self should reflect the outer universe.

[2] We should also be able to reach a similar conclusion on the Tao dynamics from other human endeavors that seek harmonious dynamic relationships. This may include fine arts, performing arts, and mathematics, etc. As we have stressed in our presentation of the Tao philosophy, quantum cosmology is only one example.

REFERENCES

AM03   R. T. Ames and D. L. Hall, "*Daodejing,*"
Balantine Books, New York, 2003

CA00   Capra, Fritjof, "*Tao of Physics,*" Shambhala Publications,
2000

CH00   Chen, Guu-Ying 陳鼓應 「老子今註今譯」
台灣台灣商務印書館, 2000

GA96   Gao Ming 高明 「帛書老子校注」 北京中華書局 1996

GE99   Genz, Henning, "*nothingness,*" translated by Karin Heusch,
Perseus Books Publishing, 1999

KE01   Ke Jong Jin 葛榮晉 「中國哲學范疇通論」
北京 首都師範大學出版社, 2001

HA01   Hawking, Stephen W., "*The universe in a nutshell,*"
Bantam Books, New York, 2001

HE89   Henricks, Robert G., "*Lao-Tzu Te Tao Ching,*"
Modern Library Edition, Random House, New York, 1989

HE00   Heidegger, Martin, "*Introduction to Metaphysics,* " English
translation by G. Fried and R. Polt, Yale University Press,
2000

KA00   Kane, Gordon, "*Supersymmetry,*"
Perseus Publishing, Cambridge, Massachusetts, 2000

KO98   Kohn, Livia and Michael LaFargue, Editors, "*Lao-tzu and
the Tao-Te-Ching,*" State University of New York Press,
1998

LA92   LaFargue, Michael, "*The Tao of the Tao Te Ching,*"
State University of New York Press, 1992

MA82   Mandelbrot, Beboit, "The Fractal Geometry of Nature," W.
H. Freeman, 1982

SA96   Sahakian and Sahakian, "*Ideas of the Great Philosophers,*"
Barnes & Noble, 1996

SM01   Smolin, Lee, "*Three Roads to Quantum Gravity,*"
Basic Books, New York, 2001

SU03	Sun, Yikai 孫以楷 「老子通論」 安微大學出版社 2003
TA92	Talbot, Michael, *The Holographic Universe*," Haper Perennial, 1992
WA58	Waley, Arthur, *The Way and Its Power*," Grove Press, New York, 1958
WA93	Wang, Po 王博 「老子思想的史官特色」 台北文津出版社, 1993
WA00	Wang, Liqi. 王利器 「文子疏義」 北京中華書局 2000
WA04	A preliminary model was published in 海峽兩岸首屆當代道 家研討會 in May, 2004 in Wuhan University 武漢大學, 2004
WU01	Wu, Yi 吳怡 「新譯老子解義」 台灣三民書局 2001
XU92	Xu, Kangsheng 許抗生著 「魏晉思想史」 台北桂冠圖書公司 1992
ZH02	Zhang, Dainian, *Key Concepts in Chinese Philosophy*," Translated by Edmund Ryden, Yale University Press 2002. 張岱年「中國古典哲學概念范範疇要論」

PART II
VERSE-BY-VERSE TRANSLATION

(精) *Its essence,*
流於天地之間 *flowing between heaven and earth,*
謂之鬼神 *is called Spirit and God.*
藏於胸中 *When concealed in the Chest, he*
謂之聖人 *is called the Sage.*

From Guantzu Inner Exercise (管子 內業篇)

Transmutation of Yo and Wu

有無相生

77

VERSE-BY-VERSE TRANSLATION

This Part contains a complete verse-by-verse translation of the Tao Te Ching based on our analysis described in Part I. Our purpose is to render an accurate translation of each verse, while maintaining coherency of each chapter and the whole book. In order to preserve the internal consistency and to avoid introducing spurious terms in the interpretation, we have retained many keywords in Chinese terms, such as Wu, Yo and Te. These terms are the main essence of Tao and any casual translation will lead to confusions. To help the readers, we have added footnotes in each Chapter for such special technical terms.

The Chinese verses are arranged so that each verse can be compared directly with its English translation.

We have added our own Chinese and English titles to reflect the central principles identified in each Chapter. The footnotes below each Chapter contain additional information related to our discussions in Part I, and serve to bring out the highlight of our interpretations. We have attempted to minimize any speculation beyond our model.

Tao may be spoken of and it is not a constant Tao;
Tao may be manifested and it is not a constant manifestation.

Tao may be described as a dynamic Tao;
Tao may be shown with dynamic manifestations.

(From Laotzu Chapter 1 Verse 1)

1   The Dynamic Tao 道可道 [1]

1	道，可道也， 非恒道也；	Tao may be spoken of and it is not a constant Tao.
2	名，可名也， 非恒名也。	Its essence may be manifested and it is not a constant manifestation.
3	無， 名萬物之始；	As Wu, it marks the beginning of all beings;
4	有， 名萬物之母。	as Yo [2], it is the mother for all beings.
5	故	Therefore,
6	恒無， 欲以觀其所妙；	As true Wu, it is to show its transmuting appearance (of Yo); [3]
7	恒有， 欲以觀其所徼。	As true Yo, it is to show its transmuting disappearance (into Wu) [4].
8	兩者同出， 異名同謂。	The two emanate from the same; they are different manifestations of the same. [5]
9	玄之又玄， 眾妙之門。	It is profound and profound. This is the gateway to all mysteries.

---

[1] **1** See Section 3 of Part I for a full interpretation of this Chapter.

[2] **1:4** We have adopted the particular form "*Yo*" to represent 有 (commonly shown as *You*). Yo is our technical term to describe the state of Yo 有.

[3] **1:6** 恒無 Constant Wu is a state of true and genuine Wu, where Wu is developed to its ultimate and where we can see how Yo state comes into being in Wu. . *Miao* 妙 is ultimate minuteness, according to Wang Bi. This verse describes the transmutation of Wu into Yo. We adopt Wang Bi's version for verses 6 and 7, without the breaking pause represented by 也.

[4] **1:7** *Jiao* 徼 is the end, return, or concealment, according to Wang Bi. This verse describes the transmutation of Yo into Wu.

[5] **1:8** The two 兩者 refers to the manifestation states of Tao as Wu and Yo. They are from the same source, which we identify as Oneness.

2　All Know Beauty 天下皆知美

1	天下	Under heaven,
2	皆知美之爲美，	all know beauty as beauty,
	惡已。	because we perceive ugliness.
3	皆知善，	All know kindness,
	斯不善矣。	because we perceive unkindness.
4	故	Therefore, (we see)
5	有無相生，	Yo and Wu come into being in each other;[1]
6	難易相成，	Hard and easy develop in each other;
7	長短相形，	Long and short come to shape in each other;
8	高下相傾。	High and low come to reflect in each other;
9	音聲相和，	Sound and sustain harmonize each other;
10	前後相隨，	Front and back follow each other.
11	恒也。	It is always so.
12	是以 聖人	The Sage
13	居無爲之事，	prefers tasks of Wu-action[2], and
	行不言之教。	conducts teachings without words.
14	万物作而弗始。	All beings proceed without showing a start,
15	爲而弗恃也，	act without expecting a return, and
16	功成而弗居也。	accomplish without showing preferences[3].
17	夫唯弗居，	Only by showing no preference,
	是以弗去。	it will never fade away.

---

[1] **2:5** Yo and Wu emerge from each other into being. See Section 3.6.

[2] **2:13** Wu-wei 無爲 is the proper actions according to Wu. See Section 4.2.

[3] **2:16** 弗居 without taking a position to show any preference; without occupying the position to display the accomplishment. Not to dwell on a preference.

3 Not Promoting Wealth 不尙賢

1	不尙賢，	Not promoting wealth[1]
	使民不爭；	keeps people from contending.
2	不貴難得之貨，	Not treasuring rare goods
	使民不爲盜；	keeps people from stealing.
3	不見可欲，	Not displaying the desirable
	使民不亂。	keeps people from chaos.
4	是以聖人之治：	Therefore, the Sage rules by
5	虛其心，	emptying the minds and
	實其腹，	filling the stomachs;
6	弱其志，	weakening the ambition and
	強其骨。	strengthening the bones.
7	恒使民	In order to guide people to the
	無知、無欲也，	Wu-wisdom[2] and Wu-desire.
8	使夫智不敢，	This keeps men of knowledge[3] refrained
	弗爲而已，	from daring, and act only with Wu.
9	則無不治矣。	Nothing is then unmanaged.

---

[1] **3:1** The word 賢 is commonly interpreted as "ability," but it should be interpreted as "wealth" or "worthiness" based on its root word 貝 that appears as part of 賢 and 貨 in this Chapter. This usage has been identified, as cited in [CH00]. The word 賢 is also used in Chapter 75 to means accumulation of wealth or surplus. See Section 9.5.

[2] **3:7** Wu-wisdom 無知 is the wisdom according to the Wu-state. See Section 4.3. Wu-Desire 無欲 is the primordial desire associated with the Wu-state.

[3] **3:8** 智 is a man with temporary knowledge, not the true wisdom. The word 智 is composed of wisdom (知) that will last only a day (日). See Section 4.4.

4   Tao Looks Empty 道沖

1	道沖， 而用之又弗盈也。	Tao looks empty. Its usefulness is never exhausted. [1]
2	淵呵 似萬物之宗。	With great depth, it seems the principle for all beings.
3	挫其銳， 解其紛；	It has blunted its sharpness, and unraveled its entanglements,
4	和其光， 同其塵；	It has harmonized its lights, and blended with its surroundings.
5	湛呵似或存。	Imperceptible, it seems existing.
6	吾不知其誰之子，	We do not know whose son it is.
7	象帝之先。	It is before the Primordial God[2].

---

[1] **4:1** Tao, as a useful vessel, remains as though always unoccupied or empty, so it can be useful all the time. When it is filled, it is no longer useful as a vessel. 沖 is not empty, but is to dilute , to flush away, to rinse, to wash away.

[2] **4:7** 象帝 Primordial God represents the first image with authority (象帝).

5　Greatest Benevolence 天地不仁

1	天地不仁， 以萬物爲芻狗；	Heaven and earth showing no benevolence treat all beings as straw-dogs[1].
2	聖人不仁， 以百姓爲芻狗。	The Sage showing no benevolence treats all people as straw-dogs.
3	天地之間， 其猶橐籥與！	Space between heaven and earth behaves like a bellows!
4	虛而不屈， 動而愈出。	It is empty but is never exhausted. It is dynamic and keeps yielding more.
5	多聞數窮， 不若守於中。	Wanting to know more leads to wit's end. One rather ponders in the center[2].

---

[1] **5:1** Any special benevolence will disturb the true nature of things. Heaven and earth show impartiality as the greatest benevolence. See also Chuangtzu Chapter 2: Greatest Benevolence shows no benevolence 大仁不仁. A sacrificial straw dog is discarded after it serves its specific divine purposes.

[2] **5:5** 多聞 is more learning or knowledge. 守於中 means as though to stay in the center with tranquility.

6   **Spirit of Valley 谷神不死**

1   谷，神，不死，   Its vastness and manifestations never die[1].
    是謂玄牝。   It is the profound source of life[2].

2   玄牝之門，   This gate of this profound source of life is
    是謂天地根。   the root of heaven and earth.

3   綿綿若存，   Ceaselessly, it seems perceptible.
    用之不勤。   Its function is inexhaustible[3].

---

[1]   **6:1** 谷 valley and 神 spirit represent the manifestations of Tao: valley 谷 represents the state of Wu as vast and deep, and god 神 represents the state of Yo, as manifestations of Tao. The interplay of Wu and Yo never ceases 不死 and acts as the life source of all beings. This interpretation is consistent with Chapter 1. The term 谷 valley and 神 spirit are also treated as separate items in **39:4 and 39:5.**

[2]   **6:1** 玄牝 is Heavenly Source of Life. 牝 is the mysterious Cow, or a female animal, which symbolizes the ultimate source of all-beings. 玄 is deep and dark, and mysterious. It represents the closest state to Tao, so we interpret it as *heavenly.*

[3]   **6:3** 用之不勤 may also mean that it may be used without exhaustion or effort.

7　Lasting Forever 天長地久

1	天長地久。	Heaven endures long and earth lasts forever.
2	天地所以能 長且久者，	Heaven and earth can endure long and last forever, because
3	以其不自生， 故能長生。	they do not live by relying on themselves[1], so they can live long.
4	是以聖人	Therefore, the Sage
5	退其身而身先， 外其身而身存。	keeps himself behind, as to lead, and forgoes himself, as to sustain.
6	非以其無私邪？ 故能成其私。	Isn't it by his selflessness[2] that he can achieve his goals for himself?

---

[1] **7:3** 自生 Self-existence. To live for or by oneself. They all rely on Tao to live. In our interpretation, heaven and earth are manifestations of Tao. They are connected to the Wu state, so they will last forever. If heaven and earth were only relying on their Yo states, they will not last long. Yo comes into being in Wu. This is echoed in Chapter 39.

[2] **7:6** Wu-Self 無私 may be identified with the Self in the Wu-state. It is a self-less state. This true Self is concealed and is one with heaven and earth. 其私 refers to his "selfish" goals. Wu-Self appears only once in Tao Te Ching.

8   The Ultimate Best 上善若水

1	上善若水。	The utmost best[1] is like water.
2	水善利萬物 而又靜。	Water best benefits all beings and retains its tranquility.
3	居眾人之所惡， 故幾於道。	It stays where others despise, so it is nearest to Tao.
4	居善地，	In dwelling, best by adapting to the place.[2]
5	心善淵，	In heart, best by showing its vastness.
6	與善仁，	In giving, best with benevolence.
7	言善信，	In words, best with trustworthiness.
8	正善治，	For rectification, best by justice.
9	事善能，	In serving, best with ability.
10	動善時。	In action, best with timeliness.
11	夫唯不爭， 故無尤。	Only by not contending, one invites no resentment.

---

[1] **8:1** 上善 is The Highest Good, or the ultimate master.

[2] **8:4** The best way to live is to fit into the place, without interrupting or disrupting the place. Otherwise, we would be contending with nature. The same interpretation follows throughout the chapter.

9   Effacing after Accomplishment 功遂身退

1	持而盈之， 不若其已。	Retaining it until overflowing is not as good as let it be naturally.
2	揣而銳之， 不可長保。	Sharpness by whittling cannot be preserved long.
3	金玉滿堂， 莫之能守。	Gold and jade accumulated in the halls cannot be protected well.
4	富貴而驕， 自遺其咎。	Wealth and nobility, when displayed, invite to oneself their calamities[1].
5	功遂身退， 天之道也。	Effacing after accomplishment[2] is the Tao of Heaven.

---

[1] **9:4** 自遺 is to leave for, or transfer to, oneself.

[2] **9:5** 身退 is to efface, to retreat or to back out. The Tao of Heaven may also be translated as the way of heaven.

10 Heavenly Te 玄德

1	載營魄抱一， 能毋離乎？	Embracing Oneness with body and soul[1], can they be kept un-separated?
2	摶氣致柔， 能嬰兒乎？	Focusing Chi to its softest state, can we reach infancy?
3	滌除玄鑒， 能毋有疵乎？	Cleansing our minds, can we become spotless?
4	愛民治國， 能無以智乎？	Caring for people and ruling a state, can we rely not on our knowledge[2]?
5	天門啓闔， 能爲雌乎？	Keeping our senses[3] attentive to outside, can we submit to nature?
6	明白四達， 能毋以知乎？	After attaining extensive knowledge, can we rely on our wisdom of Wu[4]?
7	生而弗有也， 爲而弗恃也， 長而弗宰也，	Bringing into being without possessing, acting without seeking return, and supporting without seeking control
8	是謂玄德。	are known as Heavenly Te[5].

---

[1] **10:1** The soul (營) refers to the superior soul and body (魄) to the lower soul. 抱一 is to embrace Oneness and abide with Tao.

[2] **10:4** 智 is temporary knowledge, not true wisdom. See Section 4.4.

[3] **10:5** The vital senses refer to the gates to heaven (天門). Femininity (雌) refers to source of life, submission to the nature, regeneration of life, and nativity.

[4] **10:6** This wisdom 知 is Wu-wisdom, which is the true wisdom of the Wu-state. See Section 4.4. We have interpreted 毋以知 as 無以知 to know according to the Wu state, in the way consistent with "acting with Wu" in Chapter 38.

[5] **10:8** 玄德 the Heavenly Te is also defined in Chapter 51. This chapter shows how man behaves with this heavenly te. We choose to use the term *Heavenly* to describe the ultimate state of harmony in man-heaven relationship.

11   Wu-Yo as Function 無有之用

1	卅輻共一轂， 當其無有， 車之用也。	With thirty spokes connected to the hub, it is its "Wu and Yo" that makes a wagon functional. [1]
2	埏埴而爲器， 當其無有， 器之用也。	With clay molded into a vessel, it is its "Wu and Yo" that makes a vessel functional.
3	鑿戶牖， 當其無有， 室之用也。	With doors and windows chiseled out, it is its "Wu and Yo" that makes a room functional.
4	故	Therefore,
5	有之以爲利，	Yo is to provide the support. [2]
6	無之以爲用。	Wu is to provide the function. [3]

---

[1] **11:1** Both the manifested (Yo 有) and the un-manifested (Wu 無) are equally essential in Tao. Most interpretations emphasize Wu as the essential function, but, according to our model, Wu and Yo should always be paired together to make it complete and functional.

[2] **11:5** 有之 means to purposefully show as the Yo state, or to make it an explicit manifestation.

[3] **11:6** 無之 means to purposefully show as the Wu state, or to make it an implicit manifestation.

12 For Essence 爲腹不爲目

1	五色令人目盲，	Five colors make our eyes blind.
2	馳騁田獵，	Chasing and hunting in the fields
	使人心發狂，	make our minds mad.
3	難得之貨，	Rare goods
	使人之行妨，	hinder our path.
4	五味令人口爽，	Five flavors make our palates numb.
5	五音令人耳聾。	Five tones make our ears dumb.
6	是以聖人之治也，	The rule of the Sage is to care
7	爲腹不爲目，	for the stomach and not for the eyes[1].
8	故去彼而取此。	He would not want it any other way.[2]

---

[1] **12:7** The inner need (the stomach) is essential and the outer sensations (the eyes) are superficial. Colors are superficial and make us blind to the essence of Tao.

[2] **12:8** A literal translation is "He would discard others to choose this." The sage would not want to have it any other way.

13 Favor and Disfavor 寵辱若驚

1	寵辱若驚， 貴大患若身。	Favor and disfavor startle us, as though a disaster falling upon us.
2	何謂寵辱若驚？	Why "favor and disfavor startle us"?
3	寵之爲下。	Giving favor is an act of humbleness[1],
4	得之若驚， 失之若驚，	but we are still startled to get it and startled to lose it.
5	是謂 寵辱若驚。	This is what we mean by "favor and disfavor startle us."
6	何謂 貴大患若身？	Why should this be regarded as "a disaster falling upon us? "
7	吾所以有大患者， 爲吾有身也。	We are beset by such a disaster because we have concern for Self.
8	及吾無身， 吾有何患？	If we have no Self[2], we are free from disasters.
9	故	Therefore.
10	貴爲身於 爲天下， 若可以託天下矣；	Treat ourselves is best to treat it for all under heaven[3], as though we can care for all under heaven.
11	愛以身 爲天下， 如可寄天下矣。	Endear and submit ourselves to all under heaven[4], as though we can depend on all under heaven.

---

[1] **13:3** 爲下 also appears in Chapter 61.

[2] **13:8** Without Self 無身 is to be without concerns for self, in the state of Wu.

[3] **13:10** The best way 貴 to consider for ourselves 爲身 is to consider ourselves for the world 爲天下, as though we are going to take care of all under heaven. We should consider ourselves beyond the trivia of favor and disfavor of ourselves.

[4] **13:11** We should endear 愛 or submit ourselves 以身 to contribute to the world 爲天下 as though we can depend on all under heaven. We should not endear ourselves for ourselves; otherwise, we will be concerned about ourselves.

14   The Threads of Tao   道紀

1	視之而弗見， 名之曰微；	Looking at it, we cannot see it. We describe it as invisible.
2	聽之而弗聞， 名之曰希；	Listening to it, we cannot hear it. We describe it as inaudible.
3	昏之而弗得， 名之曰夷。	Touching it, we cannot feel it. [1] We describe it as imperceptible.
4	三者不可致詰， 故混而爲一。	These three cannot describe it, so they are merged into one.
5	一者，	This one,
6	其上不皦，	while high up, is not bright;
7	其下不昧。	while deep down, is not dark.
8	繩繩不可名也， 復歸於無物。	Ceaselessly, it is beyond description. It reverts to nothingness. [2]
9	是謂無狀之狀，	It is a form with no form.
10	無物之象， 是謂惚恍。	As an image with no object, it is shown as fleeting disappearances and appearances. [3]
11	隨之不見其後； 迎之不見其首。	Following it, we do not see its back. Welcoming it, we do not see its front.
12	執今之道， 以御今之有， 以知古始。	It is by holding the Tao of today to observe the phenomena of today, that we may know its ancient beginning. [4]
13	是謂道紀。	It is known as the Threads of Tao. [5]

---

[1] **14:3** 昏 is to touch or to caress 撫

[2] **14:9** 不可名 is indescribable and beyond description as in 不可名狀.

[3] **14:10** 惚恍 is sudden absent-mindedness and sudden insights.

[4] **14:12** The verses above are descriptions of the Wu state that never change so the fundamental principles of Tao is still functioning today. The affairs of today are the Yo 有 of today, which is always coupled with the holistic Wu state. This seems to indicate that Yo may change but the connection to Wu remains unchanged. Wang Bi version has 執古之道.

[5] **14:13** 道紀 is the rules or the principles of Tao.

15   Master of Tao 善爲道者

1	古之善爲道者，	The ancient who have mastered Tao
2	微妙玄達，	are subtle and attain the ultimate, and
	深不可識。	are profound beyond comprehension.
3	夫唯不可識，	Since they are beyond our comprehension,
	故強爲之容：曰	we reluctantly describe their appearances as:
4	豫焉	Hesitant, as though
	若冬涉水；	fording across a river in the winter;
5	猶呵	Vigilant, as though
	其若畏四鄰；	being afraid of neighbors;
6	儼呵其若客；	Dignified, as though a guest;
7	渙呵其若淩釋；	Ready to disappear, as though thawing ice;
8	敦呵其若樸；	Sincere, as though simplistic;[1]
9	混呵其若濁；	Turbid, as though murky water;
10	曠呵其若谷。	Expansive, as though a valley.
11	濁而	His murkiness, through tranquility, will be
	靜之徐清；	restored gently back to clarity.
12	安以	His stagnation, through initiation, will be
	動之徐生。	brought gently back into liveliness.
13	保此道	Those who follow this Tao
	不欲盈。	do not desire to overflow.[2]
14	是以能	So, they would rather remain
	蔽而不成。	concealed and avoid reaching an end.[3]

---

[1] **15:8** Pu 樸 is the state of Pu (simplicity). It is genuine, but is in the state before showing. See Section 5.4.

[2] **15:13** 不欲盈 Do not desire to be filled to the brim, to be full. or to be overflowing. When a vessel is overflowing, it is no longer useful as a vessel. If it is overflowing, it is revealed.

[3] **15:14** 蔽而不成 He would rather remain concealed and avoid showing his accomplishment. 成 means completion of a function, so the function is no longer useful. 不成 is to avoid coming to an end, so the function can continue. See a similar use of 成 in Section 5.8.

16   Return to the Root 復歸其根

1	致虛極也， 守靜篤也。	Achieving the utmost emptiness and remaining in genuine tranquility,
2	萬物並作， 吾以觀其復也。	all beings flourish, and we observe their recurrences.
3	夫物芸芸， 各復歸其根。	The multitudes show vast varieties, but each will return to its own root.
4	歸根曰靜，	Returning to the root gains tranquility.
5	靜，是謂復命，	With tranquility, we reconcile with destiny[1].
6	復命常也，	Reconciling with destiny is nature.[2]
7	知常明也。	Knowing nature leads to enlightenment.
8	不知常，妄。	Not knowing nature leads to recklessness.
9	妄作，凶。	Recklessness invites calamity.
10	知常容， 容乃公，	Knowing nature becomes receptive. Being receptive becomes impartial.
11	公乃王， 王乃天，	Being impartial becomes all-encompassing[3]. All-encompassing is like heaven.
12	天乃道， 道乃久，	Heaven is like Tao and Tao is forever.
13	沒身不殆。	All remain concealed and never perish.

---

[1] **16:5** 復命 is Revival of the natural decree. Returning to the destiny. Submission to the fate.

[2] **16:6** This chang 常 is used in Chapter 16, 52, and 56 (Mawangdui version) to mean the unchanging naturalness of heaven and earth. The changes in other chapters mean constancy. It is the law of nature.

[3] **16:11** 王 means covering all aspects. According to 說文, 王 is where all under heaven belong to, or return to, for guidance: 王, 天下所歸往也. In addition, 王 is the son-of-Heaven (天子) who is the divine mediator of man and heaven. See also Verses **25:9** and **66:1**.

17   We followed Tzujan 我自然

1	太上， 下知有之；	Under the best condition[1], people know it and follow it.
2	其次，親譽之；	Next, people love and praise it.
3	其次，畏之；	Next, people are afraid of it.
4	其下，侮之。	Under the worse condition, people despise it.
5	信不足， 安有不信。	If we do not have enough faith in it, we will lose our faith.[2]
6	悠呵其貴言也。	Restfully, (Tao) rarely articulates.
7	成功、 遂事，	After its goals achieved and its tasks completed,
8	而百姓皆謂 我自然。	people just claim, "We followed Tzujan[3] (nature)."

---

[1] **17:1** 太上 means the best. It may refer to the state of the man-heaven relationship or the way people look at Tao. 下知有之 means the people (下) have the wisdom (知) to follow it, using Tao as the guide for the Yo state (有之).

[2] **17:5** We do not always trust Tao because we do not have enough trust in Tao. When we do not have enough trust, we will surely lose the trust. Tao, however, is always functioning without any demand. Similar sentence structure is used in verse **20:4**.

[3] **17:8** Tzu-Jan 自然 is commonly translated as "nature." It is, however, not the nature of the physical world, but is the spiritual naturalness. Tzu-Jan (自然) is the primordial unperturbed process of self-development. It is the state of Oneness. Self-So. Spontaneity. Naturally so. With no apparent reason.

18   Ruin of Tao 大道廢 [1]

1	故大道廢，	When the Great Tao is ruined,
	安有仁義。	benevolence and righteousness will appear.
2	智慧出，	When knowledge is exhausted[2],
	安有大偽。	daring propositions will appear.
3	六親不和，	When family rivalry is rampant,
	安有孝慈。	filial piety and compassion will appear.
4	邦家昏亂，	When a country is in turmoil,
	安有貞臣。	royal ministers will appear.

---

[1] **18** This chapter reflects an essential property of Tao philosophy that there is always a supporting level from which to recover to the Oneness state. The hierarchy of the Yo states represent different ways to recover from deviations from the Oneness state, as discussed in Section 3.4.When Tao is ruined, we enter into another level of Yo state in order to revert to the Oneness state again. The next best level actions still have the reverting power to restore to the higher state.

[2] **18:2** 智慧 is knowledge. Knowledge (智) and Wisdom (知) are discussed in Section 4.3. In order to gain consistency in the Chapter, we have interpreted this verse as to mean that, even when we have lost the benefit of knowledge (in the Yo state), people will resort to pretense of having admirable knowledge and try to recover from the gross deviations from Oneness. We literally interpret 出 as "out" to mean no longer there.

19　Excel in Sageness　絕聖棄智

1	絕聖棄智， 民利百倍；	Excel in Sageness and go beyond knowledge, [1] people will benefit a hundredfold.
2	絕仁棄義， 民復孝慈；	Excel in benevolence and go beyond righteousness, people will restore filial affections.
3	絕巧棄利， 盜賊無有。	Excel in craftsmanship and go beyond profiting, thievery will not manifest.
4	此三言也， 以爲文未足。	These three statements are only examples and are not sufficient. [2]
5	故 令之有所屬：	Therefore, we must seek their principles:
6	見素抱樸，	Show plainness and embrace Pu (simplicity); [3]
7	少私而寡欲。	Diminish selfishness and subdue desires;
8	絕學無憂。	This is true learning without anxieties. [4]

---

[1] **19:1** 絕 is taken to be *to excel*. It means extremely, absolutely, matchlessly, or unparalleled, so 絕聖 is to excel and reach the true state of Sageness. We use the same interpretation for 絕仁, 絕巧, and 絕學. The word 棄 is *to abandon* or *to go beyond*. Our interpretation is consistent with our positive proposition of Tao in Sageness and true learning. This chapter describes the Wu state, where we shall not seek the guidance from the Sages and we shall not rely on the knowledge of the Yo state.

[2] **19:4** 以爲文 as superficial. External. Ornaments. Appearance.

[3] **19:6** Pu 樸 is the true Wu state where Yo is germinating or concealed. It is the state that is beyond all things that are related to the Yo state – such as Sageness, knowledge, Jen, Yi, etc. See Section 5.4.

[4] **19:8** This is the ultimate learning and there will be no anxiety.

20   Seek Nourishing Source 貴食母

1	唯之與呵， 其相去幾何？	Yes and no, how different are they?
2	美與惡， 其相去何若？	Love and hatred, how different are they?
3	人之所畏， 亦不可以不畏人。	Whatever we create fear for, will inevitably become fear for us.[1]
4	荒呵，其未央哉！	How absurd, there is no end to this.
5	眾人熙熙， 若饗於太牢， 而春登臺。	People are frenzied, as if enjoying a splendid banquet and, as if celebrating the Spring on a terrace.
6	我泊焉未兆；	I, undisturbed, perceive no omen,
7	如嬰兒未咳；	like an infant showing no inclination
8	儽呵，似無所歸。	Laid-back, not belonging to anywhere.
9	眾人皆有餘， 我獨遺。	People possess abundantly; alone I am lacking.
10	我愚人之心也! 沌沌呵。	I have the heart of a fool[2] and remain untainted.
11	俗人昭昭， 我獨若昏呵。	People exhibit sparkling cleverness; alone I seem inept.
12	俗人察察， 我獨悶悶呵。	People exhibit keen scrutiny; alone I seem undemanding.
13	忽呵，其若海， 恍呵，若無所止。	Disappearing, it fades into oblivion; appearing, it prevails with no bound.
14	眾人皆有以， 我獨頑以鄙。	People display what they have; alone I am persistent to be lowly.
15	我欲獨異於人， 而貴食母。	Alone am I different from others and adore the nourishing mother[3].

---

[1] **20:3** This is similar to the structure in verse **17:5**.

[2] **20:10** 愚人之心 is a heart with no desire, the state of Pu. See Section 5.4.

[3] **20:15** 食母 is the nourishing mother or the source of life. It refers to Tao.

21　The Incipient Te 孔德之容

1	孔德之容， 惟道是從。	The manifestation of Incipient Te[1] follows Tao exactly.
2	道之物， 唯恍唯惚。	Tao, when perceptible, is like fleeting appearances and disappearances.
3	惚呵恍呵， 中有象呵。	Disappearing and appearing,[2] there is an image within.
4	恍呵惚呵， 中有物呵。	Appearing and disappearing, there is substance within.
5	窈呵冥呵， 其中有情呵。	Hidden and concealed, there is essence within.[3]
6	其情甚真， 其中有信。	Its essence is authentic; there is truth within.
7	自今及古， 其名不去，	From now to the ancient times, its manifestations never cease.
8	以順眾父。	It adheres to the source of all-beings.[4]
9	吾何以知 眾父之然，	How do we understand the nature of this source of all-beings?
10	以此。	By the appearance of the Incipient Te.[5]

---

[1] **21:1** 孔德 We have associated the Incipient Te in the Wu state, which follows Tao exactly as in the Oneness state. This chapter describes how Tao manifests in the Wu state. 容 is 容動 as an appearance, a gentle process or motion.

[2] **21:3** 惚恍 is a fleeting undulation of disappearing (惚) and appearing (恍). It is vague and elusive. See Uncertainty Principle.

[3] **21:5** 情 is truthfulness. It is also 精 the essence, vitality, spirit, precise, exquisite, etc. The essence is later associated with Chi as 精氣.

[4] **21:8** 眾父 variation of 眾甫. The beginning or initiation of all beings.

[5] **21:10** 以此 means "by this." This refers to the first verse, the appearance of Incipient Te 孔德.

22 Revert to Wholeness 曲則全 [1]

1	曲則全，	Twist will revert (again) to wholeness. [2]
	枉則直；	Crook will revert to uprightness.
2	窪則盈，	Shallow will revert to overflowing.
	敝則新；	Exhaustion will revert to renewal.
3	少則得，	Loss will revert to gain.
	多則惑。	Excess will revert to decline. [3]
4	是以聖人執一，	Therefore, the Sage holds fast to Oneness
	以爲天下牧。	to guide all under heaven. [4]
5	不自見故明；	By not self-showing, he is enlightening.
6	不自是故彰；	By not self-asserting, he is conspicuous.
7	不自伐故有功；	By not self-boasting, he has merit.
8	弗矜故能長。	By not self-glorifying, he sustains.
9	夫唯不爭，	Because he does not contend, nothing in the
	故莫能與之爭。	world can contend against him.
10	古之所謂	When the ancient said,
	曲全者，	"twist vs. wholeness,"
	豈語哉！	These were not just (hollow) words!
11	誠全而歸之。	One should earnestly return to this principle.

---

[1] **22** Verses 1-3 are description of the nature with reverting power to preserve Oneness, so a Sage will not contend with such nature. Minor errors should be treated as eclipses on enlightenment and should not become burdens.

[2] **22:1** This interpretation is best shown by Wentzu 文子上義: To allow minor twisting in order to preserve the long stretch 屈寸而申尺, and to allow minor wrongs to preserve great uprightness 小枉而大直，This is what a Sage would do 聖人爲之。 "Minor errors should not become a burden 雖有小過，不以爲累也。 Also" Errors of man of integrity is like an eclipse of enlightenment 君子之過，猶明之蝕 should not harm his enlightenment 不害於明。

[3] **22:3** 多 is to collect more, as in 多。 The word 惑 means great cost 大費 and decline 厚亡。 See also Chapter 44. 多藏必厚亡。

[4] **22:4** Oneness will automatically harmonize or guide the interplay of the two *opposites* in the above verses. If Oneness is followed, the balance will be achieved by itself.

23 Nature seldom articulates 希言自然

1	希言自然。	Nature seldom articulates. [1]
2	飄風不終朝，	Gusty winds do not last a morning;
	暴雨不終日。	Torrential rains do not last a day.
3	孰爲此。	This is definitely the way.
4	天地而弗能久，	Heaven and earth cannot uphold long;
	而況於人乎？	How can men?
5	故從事而	Therefore, our efforts should,
6	道者同於道；	while in Tao, synchronize with Tao;
7	德者同於德；	while in Te, synchronize with Te;
8	失者	in a lost state,
	同於失。	synchronize with the lost state. [2]
9	同於德者，	For those synchronized with Te,
	道亦德之；	Tao will work (effectively) in Te.
10	同於失者，	For those synchronized with the lost state,
	道亦失之。	Tao will work in the lost state. [3]

---

[1] **23:1** 希言 is prudent in teaching specific rules or instructions. Nature, i.e. Tzujan 自然, is not to insist on its own way, but to follow the surrounding condition closely (as expressed in this chapter). This is opposite of Verse 5:5 多言數窮。

[2] **23:8** To be effective or for Tao to be effective in a state, one must always be in harmony with the existing state. Even in a lost state (失者), Tao will function in the lost state, if we identify with the lost state. As to be in synchronization.

[3] **23:10** Tao will appear (as the Yo state) differently to different people in different states and work effectively. People should synchronize with their surrounding state and seek the synchronization signals in that state. See Section 3.10.

24   Tiptoe cannot be Firm 企者不立

1	企者不立，	Standing on tiptoes cannot be firm.
3	自是者不彰，	He who asserts himself will not be conspicuous.
2	自見者不明，	He who shows himself will not be enlightening.
4	自伐者無功，	He who boasts about himself will have no merit.
5	自矜者不長。	He who glorifies himself cannot sustain long. [1]
6	其在道也，	This is according to Tao.
7	曰：	These are like:
	餘食贅行。	food leftover or gestures unwanted. [2]
8	物或惡之，故	They are disliked, so
	有道者弗居。	man with Tao avoids them. [3]

---

[1] **24:5** 自矜者 One with self-importance. With vanity, arrogance, conceit, superiority.

[2] **24:7** 贅行 also appears as 贅形. Extraneous and abnormal growth or deformed growth. Unnatural gesture.

[3] **24:8** 有道者 is written as 有裕者 in the Mawangdui version.

25   Tao adheres to Nature 道法自然

1	有物混成， 先天地生。	With chaotic substances, it exists before heaven and earth.
2	寂呵寥呵， 獨立而不改，	Silent and scant, it stands independently without change.
3	可以爲天地母。	It is the mother of heaven and earth.
4	吾不知其名， 字之曰道。	We do not know its name, and call it Tao.
5	吾強爲之 名曰大。	We reluctantly describe it as immense. [1]
6	大曰逝， 逝曰遠，	Immensity will sustain. Sustenance will reach far.
7	遠曰返。	Reaching far will return.
8	道大，天大， 地大，	Tao is immense; heaven is immense; earth is immense, and
9	王亦大。	its compassion [2] is also immense.
10	國中有四大， 而王居一焉。	Among four immense in the universe, its encompassing nature is most important.
11	人法地， 地法天，	Man follows earth. Earth follows heaven.
12	天法道， 道法自然。	Heaven follows Tao. Tao follows Tzujan.

---

[1] **25:1** Immense is limitless, vast, and without boundary.

[2] **25:9** See note for 王 in verses 16:11 and 66:1. 王 is the encompassing nature of Tao. We may also infer from this, that 王 is the leader of man who has compassion for all.

26　Heaviness as Anchor 重爲輕根

1　重爲輕根，　　Heaviness is the anchor for lightness.
　　靜爲躁君。　　Tranquility is the control of restlessness.

2　是以君子　　Therefore, a man of integrity[1]
　　終日行，　　executes his daily tasks without
　　不離其輜重。　departing from his anchoring base.

3　雖有營觀，　　In spite of splendors,
　　燕居則超若。　he remains reposeful and detached.

4　奈何萬乘之主，Why would a lord of mighty power
　　而以身　　　choose to discount
　　輕於天下？　his own significance under heaven?[2]

5　輕則失本，　　Acting lightly, he will lose his anchor.
　　躁則失君。　　Acting restlessly, he will lose his control.

---

[1]　**26:2** 君子 Man of Integrity. Wang Bi text has the Sage (聖人). 文子上義：
「治之本仁義也，其末法度也. 先本後末謂之君子

[2]　**26:4** A lord would treat himself as the lightest (most insignificant) under the
heavens. This is the way to connect to his true anchor (Tao). Acting lightly or
restlessly will deviate from Tao.

27 Best Walkers 善行者無轍跡

1	善行者無轍跡；	Best travelers leave no trace.[1]
2	善言者無瑕讁。	Best teachings leave no blemish.[2]
3	善數者不用籌策。	Best calculations use no algorithm.
4	善閉者無關鑰 而不可啓也；	Best locks have no latch, so they cannot be opened.
5	善結無繩約 而不可解也。	Best ties have no knot, so they cannot be untied.
6	是以聖人	The Sage, therefore,
7	恒善救人， 而無棄人。	always helps his people, and abandons no one.
8	物無棄材， 是謂襲明。	To abandon no one, is to follow (true) illumination.
9	故	Therefore,
10	善人，善人之師；	A master is a teacher for other masters.
11	不善人， 善人之資也。	A non-master is where a master can learn from.[3]
12	不貴其師， 不愛其資， 雖智乎大迷，	Not honoring a teacher or not valuing the lessons leads us far astray, despite with knowledge.
13	是謂妙要。	This is the Essential Initiation.[4]

---

[1] **27:1** The traces are marks that deviate from nature. If actions are following the nature, then there will be no traces. Chuangtzu 莊子外篇，天地第十二:「行而無跡，事而無傳。」

[2] **27:2** Teaching should fit the situation. Tao is to synchronize with any state so there is no over corrections due to teaching.

[3] **27:12** Wang Bi noted on Chapter 49,「The able give and the needy take 能者與之.資者取之。」In Wentzu 文子上仁篇:「Those good at Tao 善用道者，will learn from others to achieve and use their ability to compensate their inability 乘人之資以立功，以其所能託其所不能也。」

[4] **27:13** 妙要 is written as 要妙 in Wang Bi version. 妙 is minute showing.

28 The Grand System 大制無割

1	知其雄，守其雌， 爲天下溪。	Knowing yang and preserving yin,[1] (Chi) flows like a divine creek.
2	爲天下溪， 恒德不離。	Being a divine creek, its true Te never departs.
3	恒德不離， 復歸於嬰兒。	When True Te never departs, all return to Infancy.
4	知其榮，守其辱， 爲天下谷。	Knowing honor and preserving disgrace, (Our heart) acts like a divine valley.
5	爲天下谷， 恒德乃足。	Being a divine valley, its true Te will be abundant.
6	恒德乃足。 復歸於樸。	With abundant true Te, all return to Pu.
7	知其白，守其黑， 爲天下式。	Knowing white and preserving black, (The Sage) holds it like a divine rule.[2]
8	爲天下式， 恒德不忒。	Being a divine rule, its true Te never loses its ability.
9	恒德不忒， 復歸於無極。	When true Te never loses its ability, all return to the Ultimate Wu (Oneness).
10	樸散則爲器。	Pu diffuses to mold (man into) vessels.[3]
11	聖人用則爲官長。	The Sage uses this to function as a leader.
12	故 大制無割。	Thus, the Grand System is not fragmented.[4]

---

[1] **28:1** The creek under heaven 天下溪 behaves as a triggering state of Tao.

[2] **28:7** 天下式 refers to the guiding principle of the Oneness state. See Verse 22:4, where holding to Oneness is the function of the Sage.

[3] **28:10** The Pu 樸 of Tao disperses into all beings, which will then have form and become the vessels of Tao. 文子: 道散爲萬物，物先有形而後成器.

[4] **28:12** The Grand system of Tao is supported by the reverting nature of Chi, man as vessels, and the Sage as the leader. See Section 5.4 for discussion of this Chapter.

29 World as Vessels of Tao 天下神器

1	將欲 取天下而爲之，	One may wish to conquer all under heaven and act upon it.
2	吾見其弗得已。	I see that the goal cannot be attained.
3	夫天下神器也， 非可爲者也。	All under heaven are vessels of Tao[1], and should not be acted upon.
4	爲之者敗之， 執之者失之。	Whoever acts on it will cause failure, and whoever steers it will cause deviation,[2]
5	故物	Therefore, it is natural that
6	或行或隨；	some will lead and some will follow;
7	或嘘或吹；	some will hush and some will whoop;
8	或強或羸；	some will conquer and some will win;
9	或培或墮。	some will grow and some will fail.
10	是以聖人 去甚，去泰， 去奢。	Therefore, the Sage will just remove extremes, excesses, and extravagance.

---

[1] **29:3** 神器 – The world is a vessel 器 for the manifestation 神 of Tao.

[2] **29:4** 執者 is one who insists on a particular way. This verse also appears in Verse **64:7**.

30 Best is just to resolve 善者果而已

1	以道佐人主， 不以兵強於天下。	Whoever guides a lord with Tao will not rely on armies to dominate the world.
2	其事好還。	Such actions often invite retaliations.
3	師之所居， 荆棘生之。	Wherever troops are deployed, thistles and thorns spread.
4	善者果而已矣， 毋以取強焉。	The best is just to bring a result only[1], and is not to gain power.
5	果而毋驕，	With a result, without arrogance,
6	果而勿矜，	With a result, without pride, and
7	果而勿伐。	With a result, without boasting.
8	果而毋得已居， 是謂果而不強。	Decisiveness as the last resort only.[2] It is a result without showing strength.
9	物牡而老， 是謂之不道， 不道早已。	Strength, when displayed, leads to decline and is against Tao.[3] Whatever is against Tao will perish early.

---

[1] **30:4** Best to have result only 善者果. Seeking to settle only (not to win). It is to have fruition as completion or an end. 果 also means decisiveness. Once the result is there, it should stop 而已.

[2] **30:8** 毋得已 is 不得已 in Wang Bi version. With reluctance, allowing for an imperfection. As the last resort. 居 is taken to be 者; this word makes the phrase 毋得已者 as a noun.

[3] **30:9** 物牡 whatever shows masculinity or strength. This verse is repeated in Verse **55:9**.

31 Instrument of ill Omen 不祥之器

1	夫兵者，不祥之器， 物或惡之，	War, instrument of ill omen, is often disliked.
2	故有道者弗居。	Man with Tao stays away from it. [1]
3	君子居則貴左， 用兵則貴右。	Man of integrity keeps daily life to the left, and war affairs to the right. [2]
4	故兵者 非君子之器也。	So, war is not an instrument for man of integrity.
5	兵者不祥之器也， 不得已而用之。	War is an instrument of ill omen, and is used only as the last resort.
6	恬淡爲上， 勿美也。	It should be done without ambition, and without glory.
7	若美之， 是樂殺人也。	Glorifying it is to celebrate killing.
8	夫樂殺人，不可以 得志於天下矣。	Those who celebrate killing could not sustain success under heaven.
9	是以吉事上左， 喪事上右。	We honor the left for auspicious affair, and honor the right for a funeral. [3]
10	是以 偏將軍居左， 上將軍居右。	That is why lieutenant generals stay to the left, and senior generals to the right.
11	言以喪禮居之也。	This is because we treat it as a funeral.
12	殺人眾， 以悲哀蒞之，	For the multitude killed, we mourn with sorrow.
13	戰勝而 以喪禮處之。	For a war victory, we observe it as a funeral.

---

[1] **31:2** 有道者 is written as 有裕者 in the Mawangdui version.

[2] **31:3** Prefers the left side 貴左 is a Chinese custom to consider the left as a higher honor position than the right.

[3] **31:9** In war ceremony, the left is no longer auspicious or honored. 喪禮 and 喪事 are funerals, an inauspicious affair.

32 Pu and the Tao System 樸與制

1	道恆無， 名樸。	When Tao manifests as true Wu, it is called Pu (Simplicity). [1]
2	雖小， 而天下弗敢臣。	It is minute, but cannot be subdued by anyone under heaven.
3	侯王若能守之， 萬物將自賓。	If a lord can adhere to it, all beings will assume their natural places.
4	天地相合， 以雨甘露，	Heaven and earth will harmonize and will rain with sweet dews.
5	民莫之令 而自均焉。	People, under no mandate, will self-balance.
6	始制 有名，	When a system is started, it manifests as Yo. [2]
7	名亦既有， 夫亦將知止，	When its manifest is established, it will also automatically knows when to stop. [3]
8	知止所以不殆。	It knows when to stop, so it will never end.
9	譬道之在天下也， 猶小谷 之與江海也。	The way Tao contributes to the world is like the way little creeks contribute to the rivers and oceans.

---

[1] **32:1** We may simply say that "When Tao is manifested as true Wu 恆無, it is called Pu 樸." This is a formal definition of Pu (Simplicity). See discussion in Section 5.4.

[2] **32:6** Starting a system of order 始制 is by following Tao's full manifestations as Yo 有名。 (See also **28:12**.) This is the counterpart of the first part of the chapter, where Tao manifests as Wu. Knowing when to stop 知止 means knowing to refrain from excessiveness.

[3] **32:7** This process of self-rectification is described in Chapter 37.

33 Self-Wisdom is Illumination 自知者明

1 知人者智也，　　　　Knowing others is knowledge. [1]
　　自知者明也。　　　　Knowing oneself is enlightenment.
2 勝人者有力也，　　　Overcoming others shows forces.
　　自勝者強也。　　　　Overcoming oneself shows strength.
3 知足者富也。　　　　Knowing contentment has wealth.
　　強行者有志也。　　　Having inner control has will. [2]
4 不失其所者久也，　　Not losing one's place will endure.
　　死而不亡者壽也。　　Dying without deviation will live long. [3]

---

[1] **33:1** This chapter shows the contrast of outward and inward actions. Wisdom is inward and knowledge is outward. It also shows the differences in the Yo state and the Oneness state.

[2] **33:3** 強行者 is one who can deny or force himself with inner persistence and inward control. Contentment and wealth are outward qualities

[3] **33:4** 死而不亡 to die physically, but not to be dead spiritually. The true death 亡 is deviation from Tao. To decease without perishing.

34   Tao Overflows 道氾

1	道氾呵， 其可左右也。	Tao overflows, reaching left and right,
2	成功遂事 而弗名有也；	achieving goals and completing tasks, without showing its efforts. [1]
3	萬物歸焉 而弗爲主。	All beings return to it and it claims no lordship;
4	則恒無 欲可名於小。	It remains with true Wu, in order to show its Smallness. [2]
5	萬物歸焉 而弗爲主， 可名於大。	All beings return to it and it claims no lordship, in order to manifest its Greatness. [3]
6	是以聖人之 能成大也，	This is also the way the Sage accomplishes his greatness.
7	以其不爲大也， 故能成大。	He never shows his greatness, so he can accomplish his greatness. [4]

---

[1] **34:2** *Not to show Yo* 弗名有 and *not to control* 弗爲主 are two characteristics of Tao discussed in this chapter. 名有 is to manifest what has been accomplished.

[2] **34:4** We make the same observation as in Chapter 1 where we disassociate Wu 無 and desire 欲. This seems to be a much more coherent interpretation.

[3] **34:5** Verses 3-4 show the way Tao act to receive all beings, and the Verse 5 is a declaration of Tao's true greatness. Tao acts with its smallness as the way to accomplish its greatness.

[4] **34:7** To accomplish some great plan, we have to carry out the small sub-plans, 爲大乎其細也, as discussed in Chapter 63 and act with Wu-actions and Wu-desires.

35   Great Image 執大象

1 執大象， 天下往。	With the Great Image, [1] all under heaven will follow.
2 往而不害， 安平太。	Come to it without hindrance. [2] There will be peace and prosperity.
3 樂與餌， 過客止。	(It is like) music and food that induce passers-by to stop.
4 故道之出言也， 曰淡乎其無味也。	When Tao is offered, [3] it is insipid and flavorless.
5 視之不足見也， 聽之不足聞也，	Looking at it, it is invisible. Listening to it, it is inaudible.
6 用之不可既也。	But, when used, it is never exhausted. [4]

---

[1] **35:1** The great image is Tao. Also used in Chapter 41.

[2] **35:2** 安 is then. The Sage will lead the people to follow Tao or people will follow Tao without any hindrance.

[3] **35:4** 道之出言 when Tao is spoken of or described.

[4] **35:6** 不可既 may also mean: It never makes one full in the stomach. It is not filling. Man has abundant need for the Tao. On the contrary, food and music may be exhausted or become filling.

36 Twilit Insight 微明

1	將欲翕之，	For it to shrink,
	必固張之；	it is kept expanded.[1]
2	將欲弱之，	For it to weakens,
	必固強之；	it is kept strengthened.
3	將欲去之，	For it to eradicate,
	必固舉之；	it is kept upheld.
4	將欲奪之，	For it to be fetched,
	必固予之。	it is kept loose.
5	是謂微明。	This is called Twilit Insight.[2]
6	柔弱勝強。	Rather be weak than strong.[3]
7	魚不可脫於淵，	Fish should not leave the deep stream.
8	國利器	Important instruments of a country
	不可以示人。	should not be revealed.[4]

---

[1] **36:1** For anything to happen there must be a potential built up within and concealed. This is an example of the reverting action of nature.

[2] **36:5** Twilit, adj. Lit by twilight. Subtle light.

[3] **36:6** This verse is literally: the soft and weak will overcome the strong. In order to provide a better flow of thought in this Chapter, we have interpreted it as "The true strength is kept within the soft and weak. To remain concealed with strength is better than showing the strength.

[4] **36:8** Important instrument 利器 refers to the power of Tao in managing a country. Many interpretations also refer to weapons. Revealing weapons will diminish their usefulness. Before weapons can be effectively used, they must be well hidden from the enemy. This is also the reason that Tao is always concealed.

37 World will Self-Rectify 天下將自正

1 道恒無，
名。
Tao remains as true Wu.[1]
It will manifest.

2 侯王若能守之，
萬物將自化。
If a lord can adhere to it,
all-beings will self-evolve.

3 化而欲作，
吾將鎮之以
無名之樸。
When the self-evolution is imminent,
we subdue it
with Pu[2], the un-manifested.

4 鎮之以
無名之樸，
夫將不欲。
Subduing it
with Pu, the un-manifested,
will lead to no intention.[3]

5 不欲以靜，
天下將自正。
Having no intention leads to tranquility.
All under heaven will self-rectify.

---

[1] **37:1** See Chapter 1 for 恒無. This chapter describes the initiating stage of the Yo state. See also Chapters 28 and 32. The popular phrase in Wang Bi version 道常無爲而無不爲 (Tao always acts with Wu-action and nothing is undone) is not in the Mawangdui version.

[2] **37:3** Pu 樸 is commonly translated as Simplicity. We define it in Section 5.4

[3] **37:4** 不欲 is written as 不辱, which is also used in Chapter 44.

38 Utmost Te shows no Te 上德不德

1 上德不德，
　是以有德；
Man of utmost Te will not show his Te, because he has Te.

2 下德不失德，
　是以無德。
Man of least Te will cling to Te, because he does not have Te.

3 上德無爲
　而無以爲也；
When a man of utmost Te acts with Wu-action, he acts according to Wu.[1]

4 上仁爲之
　而無以爲也；
When a man of the utmost benevolence acts, he acts according to Wu.

5 上義爲之
　而有以爲也。
When a man of utmost righteousness acts, he acts according to Yo.[2]

6 上禮爲之
　而莫之應也，
　則攘臂而扔之。
When a man of utmost propriety acts and gets no response, he throws his arms and shows.

(Chapter 38 continues next page.)

---

[1] **38:3** 無以爲 Acting with Wu is to act according to Wu. He acts truly with Wu-Actions. See Section 9.4.

[2] **38:5** 有以爲 Acting with Yo is to act according to Yo. One is acting according to the guidance provided by Tao in the Yo-state. See Section 9.4.

7	故	Therefore,
8	失道而後德，	When deviating from Tao, we rely on Te. [1]
9	失德 而後仁，	When deviating from Te, we rely on benevolence.
10	失仁 而後義，	When deviating from benevolence, we rely on righteousness.
11	失義 而後禮。	When deviating from righteousness, we rely on propriety.
12	夫禮者， 忠信之薄也， 而亂之首也。	Propriety is a sign of diminished loyalty and trust, and is an indication of chaos to come. [2]
13	前識者， 道之華也， 而愚之首也。	Without knowing this principle [3], one sees only the ornaments of Tao, and it is the beginning of ignorance.
14	是以大丈夫 居其厚而 不居其薄；	Therefore, a man of great character seeks Tao's essence and avoids its superficiality.
15	居其實而 不居其華。	Seeks Tao's substance and avoid its ornaments.
16	故去彼取此。	Therefore, he would not want it any other way.

---

[1] **38:8** When we are unable to maintain Oneness (Tao), we may rely on the Yo state (with Te). There is a hierarchy of man-heaven interaction to be observed, before chaos sets in after state of propriety 禮. See Section 3.4.Laotzu thus defines Propriety as a lost state, but not without salvation.

[2] **38:12** Wentzu 文子: Without propriety, there will be chaos below 無禮者下亂.

[3] **38:13** 前識者 is a person or an act of presuming a conclusion or knowledge without proper observation. Judging or elaborating without knowing the principles. Thing should be examined all the time. 韓非子解老篇云：「先物行，先理動，之謂前識。前識者，無緣而忘意度。」

39 Heaven Attains Oneness 天得一以清

1	昔之得一者：	These have attained Oneness:
2	天得一 以清，	Heaven attains Oneness to have its clarity.
3	地得一 以寧，	Earth attains Oneness to have its tranquility.
4	神得一 以靈，	Manifestation attains Oneness to have its power.[1]
5	谷得一 以盈，	Valley attains Oneness to have its abundance.
6	侯王得一 以爲天下正。	A lord attains Oneness to be able to rectify all under heaven.
7	其致之也，謂	They can attain this, because
8	天毋己清， 將恐裂；	Heaven does not show its full clarity, otherwise its clarity may fragment.[2]
9	地毋己寧， 將恐廢；	Earth does not show its full tranquility, otherwise its tranquility may be ruined.
10	神毋己靈， 將恐歇；	Manifestation does not show its full power, otherwise its power may diminish.
11	谷毋己盈， 將恐竭；	Valley does not show its full abundance, otherwise its abundance may be exhausted.

(Chapter 39 continues next page.)

---

[1] **39:4** 靈 refers to the effectiveness of power. The nurturing power of the manifested state (神) is responsive and effective when it is in the state of Oneness. See Section 3.6.

[2] **39:8** Heaven will not exhaustively exhibit its clarity 天毋己清. Otherwise, its clarity may fragment 將恐裂. Heaven can maintain its true clarity by abiding with Oneness, but it will not show clarity all the time or to the extreme. It is interesting to note that the phrase 天毋己清 is 天無以清 in the Wang Bi version, where the verse may be interpreted differently as: "Heaven maintains its clarity by abiding with Wu; otherwise, it will lose clarity."

118

12	侯王毋己 貴以高， 將恐蹶。	A lord does not show his full high stature, otherwise his high stature may disappear.
13	故必貴 而以賤爲本， 必高矣 而以下爲基。	Nobleness takes lowliness as its base. [1] High takes low as its support.
14	夫是以侯王自謂 孤、寡、不穀。	This is why the lord calls himself the abandoned, deserted, or useless.
15	此其賤之本與， 非也？	This is to show the base of his lowliness. It is not for any other reason.
16	故 致數譽無譽。	Therefore, striving for honors will bring no honor.
17	是故	For this reason,
18	不欲 琭琭若玉， 珞珞若石。	one does not intend to sparkle like jades, or to clatter like stones. [2]

---

[1] **39:13** Nobleness (may be symbolized as Yo) are supported by lowliness (symbolized as Wu). The symmetry of nobleness and lowliness is maintained under the control of Tao. Wentzu 文子: Nobleness and lowliness, respect and disrespect are guided by Tao 貴賤尊卑道以制之。

[2] **39:18** We have considered *sparkling like jades* and *clattering like stones* are both seeking unnecessary attention. There is no indication in the Chinese text that clattering like stones is preferred over sparkling like jades, although it has been the way most scholars have interpreted.

40 Reverting Power 反者道之動

1	反也者 道之動也；	Reverting (to Oneness) is the way Tao moves.[1]
2	弱也者 道之用也。	Softening (with Oneness) is the way Tao functions.
3	天下之物 生於有，	All beings under heaven come into being in Yo.
4	有生於無。	Yo comes into being in Wu.[2]

---

[1] **40:1** Reverting to Oneness is how the force of Tao acts on all beings, to guide all beings back into Oneness. To move is to drive forward, to impel, to advance, etc. See page 26.

[2] **40:4** The Yo (有) and Wu (無) are interpreted as two inter-dependent manifestations of Tao. They are co-produced as a pair. See page 20.

41 Learning of Tao 上士聞道

1	上士聞道， 勤能行之；	Superior scholars, upon hearing of Tao, follow it diligently.
2	中士聞道， 若存若亡；	Modest scholars, upon hearing of Tao, falter in and out of doubt.
3	下士聞道， 大笑之。	Inferior scholars, upon hearing of Tao, burst into ridiculing laughter.[1]
4	弗笑， 不足以爲道。	If not ridiculed at, it could not be Tao.
5	是以 建言有之曰：	For these are the well-known comments:
6	明道如昧； 進道如退； 夷道如纇。	Illuminating Tao seems dark. Advancing Tao seems retreating. Smooth Tao seems uneven.
7	上德如谷； 大白如辱； 廣德如不足；	The utmost Te seems empty. The greatest purity seems like a stain. The encompassing Te seems inadequate.
8	建德如偷； 質真如渝；	The fully-established Te seems yet stealthy. The truest essence seems yet shifting.
9	大方無隅； 大器免成； 大音希聲；	The greatest square has no corner. The greatest vessel looks incomplete. The greatest sound has no reverberation.
10	大象無形； 道褒無名。	The greatest image has no form. Tao is great with no manifestation.
11	夫唯道， 善始且善成。	Only with Tao, one can be good at initiation and good at completion.[2]

---

[1] **41:3** 文子道德篇: 上學以神聽，中學以心聽，下學以耳聽。 Superior learners learn with spirit; the modest learners with heart; the inferior learners with ears.

[2] **41:11** 善始且善成 may be interpreted literally as "good at beginning and good at ending." Tao is good at initiating Yo from Wu and brings Yo to greatest completion.

42   Tao begets Oneness 道生一

1   道生一，   Tao brings Oneness into being.

     一生二，   Oneness brings Two into being.

     二生三，   Two brings Three into being. [1]

2   三生萬物。   Three brings all beings into being.

3   萬物負陰而抱陽， All beings carry yin and embrace yang,

     沖氣以爲和。   blending into Chi to achieve harmony.

4   天下之所惡，   What are avoided by all are

     唯孤、寡、不轂， being abandoned, lonely, or useless.

     而王公以自名也。 But, these are what a lord call himself.

5   故物   Likewise.

6   或損之而益，   We may lessen in order to increase.

     或益之而損。   We may increase in order to lessen.

7   古人之所教，   This has been taught by the ancient,

     亦我而教人。   and also I will teach this to others.

8   故強梁者   Because whoever refuses to follow this

     不得其死，   will not reach a proper end. [2]

9   吾將以爲   I have treated this as

     學父。   the principal of all teachings. [3]

---

[1] **42:1** In our model, there are two levels of interpretation. At one level, Oneness is one, and Wu and Yo are two. Then the Three is Oneness, Wu, and Yo as a unit in Tao philosophy. At a lower level, Oneness is Chi, and yin and yang are two. The Three is Chi, yin, and yang.

[2] **42:8** 強梁者 is one who forces his own way. In this verse, it indicates anyone who wants to impose something other than the ancient teaching will not have a proper result or end.

[3] **42:9** 學父 is 教父 in the Wang Bi version. 父 means the father, the principal, or the beginning.

43 The Softest under Heaven 天下之至柔

1	天下之至柔， 馳騁天下之至堅。	The softest under heaven can dash through the hardest under heaven.
2	無有 入於無間。	Without manifestation, it enters into where there is no crevice.[1]
3	吾是以知 無爲之有益也。	We thus know the benefit of acting with Wu.
4	不言之教， 無爲之益，	Teaching without words and benefit of Wu-actions
5	天下 希能及之矣。	can seldom be matched by anything else under heaven.

---

[1] **43:1** Here we treat Wu 無 as an adjective, so Wu-Yo 無有 means "Without manifestation", or "Without substance. "

44   Fame and Self 名與身

1	名與身孰親？	Fame and Self – which is dearer? [1]
2	身與貨孰多？	Self and wealth – which is worth more?
3	得與亡孰病？	Gain and loss – which is bad?
4	是故	For such:
5	甚愛必大費；	Whatever dearly loved will consume dearly.
6	多藏必厚亡。	Whatever dearly treasured will harbor decline.
7	故	Therefore,
8	知足不辱，	To be content invites no disgrace.
9	知止不殆，	To know when to stop will endure, and
	可以長久。	it will be everlasting. [2]

---

[1] **44:1** *Ming* 名 is the true "title or name" associated with a person that the Self 身 should live up to. We translate it as fame only as common term for *Ming*.

[2] **44:9** 知止 Know when to stop and return. To be content with what we have (知足) will not bring degradation in our virtue, but to know when and where to stop (知止), i.e., to deny ourselves from actions and desires, is the true everlasting virtue. This term also appears in Chapter 32.

45 Great Achievement 大成若缺

1	大成若缺， 其用不敝。	A greatest achievement looks incomplete, so its function will never diminish.
2	大盈若盅， 其用不窮。	A greatest abundance looks unfilled, so its function will never expire. [1]
3	大直如詘，	The greatest straightness looks crooked.
4	大巧如拙，	The greatest skillfulness looks clumsy.
5	大贏如肭。	The greatest victory looks like a defeat.
6	趮勝寒， 靜勝熱。	As fire can overcome coldness, tranquility overcomes hotness. [2]
7	清靜可以 爲天下正。	(Returning to) clarity and tranquility can rectify all under heaven. [3]

---

[1] **45:2** One with great abundance acts like yet empty, so it will always have room to accommodate more. It never overflows. Once a vessel is full, the vessel's usefulness is diminished. See Section 9.5.

[2] **45:6** We adopt the word 趮 as its ancient meaning of heat from a furnace. This verse is a transition in this chapter. As the way furnace can overcome the cold, tranquility in our mind can also subdue the hotness of the world. This interpretation leads to the concluding Verse 7.

[3] **45:7** This chapter describes the great nature of Tao and how it may appear to us as incomplete, empty, crooked, and clumsy or a defeat. We associate the quality of clarity and tranquility 清靜 with Tao that will rectify all under heaven.

46 True Contentment 知足之足

1	天下有道， 卻走馬以糞。	When there is Tao under heaven, horses return to work the field. [1]
2	天下無道， 戎馬生於郊。	When there is no Tao under heaven, warhorses are raised on the borders.
3	罪莫大於可欲，	No fault is greater than seeking desires.
4	禍莫大於 不知足，	No calamity is greater than discontentment.
5	咎莫憯於欲得。	No guilt is greater than the intention to gain.
6	故知足之足， 恒足矣。	Therefore, to be content with contentment is true contentment. [2]

---

[1] **46:1** 卻 is to return or to step back. The word 糞, in modern usage, refers to dung, but here is used as to eliminate or to sow 播.

[2] **46:6** 恒 is constant, permanent and 恒足 is everlasting contentment.

47 Without Venturing Far 不出戶知天下

1	不出於戶， 以知天下。	Without stepping out the door, we may know all under heaven.
2	不窺於牖， 以知天道。	Without peeking through a window, we can see the Tao of Heaven. [1]
3	其出彌遠， 其知彌少。	The farther we venture, the less we know.
4	是以聖人	Therefore, the Sage
5	不行而知，	knows without venturing,
6	不見而明，	enlightens without showing [2], and
7	弗爲而成。	accomplishes without acting.

---

[1] **47:2** The principles of Tao can be understood without looking at the outside world. The principles are inside. The external world provides knowledge and the internal world provides wisdom.

[2] **47:6** It may also be interpreted as, a Sage understands without seeing.

48 Shedding of Knowledge 聞道日損

1 爲學者日益，
   聞道者日損。

One who seeks learning adds everyday.
One who seeks Tao sheds everyday.

2 損之又損，
   以至於無爲。

By shedding upon shedding,
one attains the state of Wu-action[1].

3 無爲而無以爲。

By Wu-action, one acts according to Wu.[2]

4 取天下也，
   恒無事。

To take over all under heaven should
always be with Wu-efforts.[3]

5 及其有事也，
   不足以取天下。

If it demands efforts, one will not be able
to control all under heaven.[4]

---

[1] **48:2** Wu-wei 無爲 is discussed in Section 4.2.

[2] **48:3** 無以爲 is literally translated as "rely on Wu in order to act." To act according to Wu. See Section 9.4.

[3] **484** 取 is to take control of or to take over to govern or control. Wu-effort 無事 is the efforts according to the Wu-state. See Section 4.7.

[4] **48:5** The leader must have the capability to manage with Wu and should not rely on Yo, as discussed on Section 5. We may interpret 有事 Yo-efforts as the efforts made in the Yo state.

49 Sage's Heart of Wu 聖人恒無心

1	聖人恒無心， 以百姓之心爲心。	The Sage maintains a heart of Wu, and takes people's hearts as his heart.[1]
2	善者善之， 不善者亦善之，	He treats the kind with kindness. He treats the unkind also with kindness.
3	德善也。	Because Te is kindness.[2]
4	信者信之， 不信者亦信之，	He trusts the trustworthy. He trusts also the untrustworthy.
5	德信也。	Because Te is trust.
6	聖人在天下，	Sage, under heaven,
7	歙歙焉， 爲天下渾心。	remains attentive and cares with his heart for all under heaven.
8	百姓皆屬耳目焉， 聖人皆孩之。	The people attend to their ears and eyes, and the sage leads them back to childhood.[3]

---

[1] **49:1** Wu-heart 無心 is a mind or a heart that acts to maintain harmony in the Wu-state. It is without one's own selfish concerns.

[2] **49:3** Te 德 is often used as "to obtain 得." So 德善 is 得善, as to obtain or reach kindness. This is the way Te includes include all, by abandoning no one. We have punctuated 「德善也」 as 「德、善也。」 which is interpreted as "Te is to be kind." The same rule applies to Verse 5, which means "Te is to be trusting."

[3] **49:8** People pay attention to what they can see and what they can hear. This means that people rely on the Yo state. A Sage therefore will guide them to simplicity (Pu) as children, or return them back as innocent children 孩之.

129

50　Beyond Death　出生入死

1	出生入死。	Emerge into life and return into death. [1]
2	生之徒十有三；	Thirteen factors lead to life. [2]
3	死之徒十有三；	Thirteen factors lead to death.
4	而民生生， 動皆之死地之， 亦十有三。	People, in seeking preservation in life, [3] move into death, also because of the thirteen factors.
5	夫何故也？	Why so?
6	以其生生也。	Because they seek preservation in life.
7	蓋聞善攝生者，	We heard of a master Life-Seeker.
8	陵行 不避兕虎，	Walking on the hills, he does not avoid rhino or tiger.
9	入軍不被甲兵。	Into the enemy, he will not be captured.
10	兕無所投其角， 虎無所措其爪， 兵無所容其刃。	Rhinos find no spot for their horns. Tigers find no spot for their claws. Armies find no spot for their blades.
11	夫何故也？	Why is this so?
12	以其無死地焉。	Because he has attained beyond death. [4]

---

[1] **50:1** Life and death are parts of Tzu-Jan, natural events. Life is from nature and death is return to nature. Death is caused by seeking too much indulgence in life.

[2] **50:2** We have followed the common classic Chinese convention to interpret 十有三 as thirteen. Various thirteen factors have been suggested by Hanfei-Tzu 韓非子 and Hoshangkong 河上公, but they are not pertinent in interpreting the essence of this Chapter.

[3] **50:4** 生生 is to live the life; to pay too much attention in life; to seek too much or indulgence in life.

[4] **50:12** He is beyond the thirteen reasons of life and death, because he is not seeking indulgence of life. He does not deviate from Tao 死而不亡, as in Chapter 33.

51 Heavenly Te 玄德

1	道生之而德畜之，	Tao brings it into being and Te protects.[1]
2	物形之	shapes as object and
	而器成之。	completes as vessel.[2]
3	是以	Therefore,
4	萬物尊道而貴德。	all beings revere Tao and honor Te.
5	道之尊也，	Reverence for Tao and
	德之貴也，	honor for Te are
6	夫莫之爵，而	not by mandate, but are
	恒自然也。	due to true Tzujan (nature).[3]
7	道生之，畜之；	Tao brings into being and protects,
8	長之，育之；	supports it and fosters,[4]
	亭之，毒之；	molds it and sets;
	養之，覆之。	nurtures it and guards.
9	生而弗有也，	Brings into being without possessing.
10	爲而弗恃也，	Acts without seeking a return.
11	長而弗宰也，	Supports without seeking control.
12	是謂玄德。	It is known as Heavenly Te.[5]

---

[1] **51:1** This chapter describes Heavenly Te, so it refers to the Oneness state. Tao brings Oneness into being and Te protects it.

[2] **51:2** Chi 器, when used as an action, refers to the process of molding into a vessel. The molding process completes it as the vessel of Tao. 器成之 is the process of embodiment of the quality as vessel of Tao that makes a person complete.

[3] **51:6** 恒自然 is following the dynamics of the naturalness (Tzu-Jan).

[4] **51:8** 長之，育之 to support and foster their body; 亭之，毒之 to define and set their character 養之，覆之。 To nourish and protect their life.

[5] **51:12** 玄德 is Heavenly Te, or the profound Te, is also defined in Chapter 10. This Chapter describes the Heavenly Te associated with Tao in the state of Oneness, while Chapter 10 describes the Heavenly Te in man.

52 Minute and Soft 見小守柔

1 天下有始，　　　All under heaven has a beginning.
　以爲天下母。　　It is the mother of all under heaven.

2 既得其母，　　　Once we recognize the mother,
　以知其子；　　　we may observe her children.[1]

3 既知其子，　　　After having known the children, we
　復守其母，　　　return to abide with the mother.
　沒身不殆。　　　We can remain concealed and never perish.

4 塞其兌，　　　　(If we) plug our desires[2] and
　閉其門，　　　　shut our gratifications,
　終身不勤。　　　our life becomes effortless.

5 啓其兌，　　　　(If we) unlock our desires and
　濟其事，　　　　intensify our efforts,
　終身不救。　　　our life becomes beyond salvation.

6 見小曰明，　　　Seeing minuteness, we gain enlightenment.
　守柔曰強。　　　Abiding by softness, we gain strength.[3]

7 用其光，　　　　Following its light,
　復歸其明。　　　we return to its enlightenment.[4]

8 毋遺身殃，　　　This will free us from disaster.

9 是謂襲常。　　　This is known as Following Nature.[5]

---

[1] **52:2** 子 is the son or children. They are manifestations (the Yo states) of the Wu state (or the Oneness state), which is called the mother in this chapter.

[2] **52:4** 兌 refers to mouth, ear, eyes, and nose as ways to satisfy desires.

[3] **52:6** We may associate smallness with the manifestations that are the children in Verse **52:2**. We may associate softness with the source, called the mother in Verse **52:1**. Smallness (or light) may also be associated with Yo (manifestations), and mother (softness) with the Wu (source) state.

[4] **52:7** The light is the manifestation (Yo) and the true essence is the enlightenment as Wu. *Ming* 明 represents the natural, undifferentiated consciousness, direct apprehension of Tao.

[5] **52:9** 襲常 is following constancy of the Oneness state, i.e., by returning to nature.

53 Great Tao is Even 大道甚夷

1	使我挈有知，	This is what I know for sure: [1]
2	行於大道，	While pursuing Great Tao,
	唯迆是畏。	we should be careful of deviations. [2]
3	大道甚夷，	Great Tao is very even, however,
	民甚好徑。	people like shortcuts.
4	朝甚除，	The royal court is kept splendid[3], while
	田甚蕪，	fields are devastated and
	倉甚虛。	granaries depleted.
5	服文綵，	They wear fabulous clothes,
	帶利劍，	carry sharp swords and
	厭飲食。	are fed up of their food.
6	資財有餘。	They accumulate wealth with surplus.
	是謂盜竽，	They are like heads of robbers. [4]
7	非道也哉。	This is certainly not Tao.

---

[1] **53:1** 挈 sure to hold. 有知 is to have the wisdom or to know.

[2] **53:2** 迆 deviation

[3] **53:4** The character 除 may also be interpreted as "corrupted." We keep it as "splendid" to maintain the symmetry with verses 5 and 6.

[4] **53:7** 盜竽 robbery leaders

54   The Best Builder 善建者

1	善建者不拔，	Master builders do not uproot. [1]
2	善抱者不脫，	Master musters do not disperse.
3	子孫 以祭祀不絕。	The offspring sustain by continuous offering to ancestors.
4	修之身， 其德乃真。	Cultivated in a person, Te shows genuineness.
5	修之家， 其德有餘。	Cultivated in a family, Te shows plentiful-ness.
6	修之鄉， 其德乃長。	Cultivated in a village, Te shows endurance.
7	修之邦， 其德乃豐。	Cultivated in a country, Te shows abundance.
8	修之天下， 其德乃博。	Cultivated in all under heaven, Te shows universality.
9	以身觀身，	We use Te for a person, to judge a person. [2]
10	以家觀家，	We use Te for a family, to judge a family.
11	以鄉觀鄉，	We use Te for a village, to judge a village.
12	以邦觀邦，	We use Te for a country, to judge a country.
13	以天下 觀天下。	We use Te for all under heaven, to judge all under heaven.
14	吾何以知 天下之然哉？	How do we know the states of all under heaven? [3]
15	以此。	By the above rule.

---

[1] **54:1** Te is built layers upon layers. Each layer may be a manifestation of a different Yo state at different level.

[2] **54:9** To observe a person by his showing of the quality of Te, i.e., genuineness, as a person. *Guan* 觀 is to observe. It may also be interpreted as to check the state of Te of a person by observing a person.

[3] **54:14** The nature of the world is built in layers from a person, a family, a village, a country and the whole world. Te is also built in layers, so lower layers should not be uprooted when upper layers are built.

55   The Abundant Te 含德之厚

1	含德之厚者， 比於赤子。	He who has abundant Te will be like an infant. [1]
2	蜂蠆虺蛇弗螫，	Poisonous insects will not bite him.
3	攫鳥猛獸 弗搏。	Birds of prey and beasts of ferocity do not grab at him.
4	骨弱筋柔 而握固，	(His) bones are weak and sinews are tender. However, his grasps are sturdy.
5	未知牝牡之會 而朘怒， 精之至也。	He is unaware of sexual union, but shows full sensations [2] because he has the ultimate essence.
6	終日號而不嗄， 和之至也。	He cries all day without becoming hoarse, because he maintains the ultimate harmony.
7	知和曰常， 知常曰明。	Harmony leads to constancy and constancy leads to enlightenment. [3]
8	益生曰祥， 心使氣曰強。	Adding to life may be auspicious, but driving Chi with our minds leads to strength. [4]
9	物壯即老， 謂之不道， 不道早已。	Once strength is shown, it leads to decay. It is against Tao. Whatever is against Tao will perish early. [5]

---

[1] **55:1** An innocent infant. 赤子 literally means a naked or crimson red infant. It is the ultimate state of innocence.

[2] **55:5** 朘 refers to penis and 朘怒 refers to erection of penis of an infant.

[3] **55:7** 知和曰常 To have the wisdom to be in harmony leads to naturalness. 知常曰明 To follow this naturalness will lead to enlightenment.

[4] **55:8** 祥 has been taken to mean *inauspicious* in a peculiar way.

[5] **55:9** This verse is repeated in Chapter 30. See Section 9.2.

56   The Wise no longer teach 知者弗言

1	知者弗言， 言者弗知。	One with wisdom no longer teaches. One who teaches shows no wisdom. [1]
2	塞其兌， 閉其門，	Flows of desire have been plugged. Doors to gratification have been shut.
3	和其光， 同其塵，	Lights have been harmonized. The world has been unified. [2]
4	挫其銳， 解其紛，	Sharpness has been blunted. Entanglements have been unraveled.
5	是謂玄同。	This is the state of Heavenly Unity. [3]
6	故不可得而親， 亦不可得而疏；	For unknown reasons, we are intimate; for unknown reasons, we are detached. [4]
7	不可得而利， 亦不可得而害；	For unknown reasons, we benefit; for unknown reasons, we hinder.
8	不可得而貴， 亦不可得而賤。	For unknown reasons, we are noble; for unknown reasons, we are lowly.
9	故爲天下貴。	This is the most valued state under heaven.

---

[1] **56:1** This Chapter is about the state of Heavenly Unity 玄同, where the wise do not need to teach anymore. We may associate this state with Wu, where teaching is unnecessary. Teaching should only be in the Yo state. Any one attempting to teach in Heavenly Unity state is ignorant or does not understand.

[2] **56:4** The word dust 塵 is commonly used to refer to the world or environs around us. In the state of harmony, we are blended with all under heaven, or the dusts.

[3] **56:5** 玄同 is the ultimate mysterious unity with heaven, so we call it the Heavenly Unity. This is a description of the Wu state.

[4] **56:6** 不可得 means "cannot be obtained or known." In the state of harmony, all will happen naturally, without a reason.

57 Rule with Uprightness 以正治國

1	以正治國，	Rule a state with uprightness.
	以奇用兵，	Deploy an army with surprises.
	以無事取天下。	Control the world with Wu-efforts. [1]
2	吾何以	How do I know
	知其然也哉？	that it should be so?
3	夫	Because:
4	天下多忌諱	When there are too many taboos,
	而民彌貧。	people become poor in spirit.
5	民多利器	When people have many trickeries, [2]
	而國家滋昏。	the country becomes corrupted.
6	人多智巧	When people rely on clever knowledge,
	而奇物滋起。	deviance becomes pervasive. [3]
7	法物滋彰，	When treasures are vastly displayed, [4]
	而盜賊多有。	thievery becomes numerous.
8	是以聖人之言曰：	So the Sage would say:
9	我無爲而民自化，	I act with Wu and people self-evolve. [5]
10	我好靜	I remain tranquil, and
	而民自正，	people self-rectify.
11	我無事	I serve with Wu, and
	而民自富；	people self-prosper.
12	我欲不欲	I remain without intention, and
	而民自樸。	people achieve Pu by themselves. [6]

---

[1] **57:1** Wu-efforts are the efforts according to the Wu state. See Section 4.7.

[2] **57:5** 利器 refers to sharp instrument as gizmo. It may be superficial knowledge.

[3] **57:6** 奇物 is of unorthodox nature. Deviations from normal.

[4] **57:7** 法物 is "valued or good items," according to Hoshangkong.

[5] **57:9** For meanings of Wu-action 無爲 and Wu-effort 無事, See Section 4.

[6] **57:12** See Section 5.4 for discussion on Pu (Simplicity).

58 Governing without Demands 其政悶悶

1	其政悶悶， 其民惇惇。	When governing is undemanding, people are sincere.
2	其政察察， 其民夬夬。	When governing is scrutinizing, people become shrewd.
3	禍，福之所倚；	A misfortune is where a fortune lies;
4	福，禍之所伏，	a fortune is where a misfortune hides.
5	孰知其極？	How do we know its ultimate rule?
6	其無正也，	We would not know its rule.
7	正復爲奇， 善復爲妖，	Uprightness may re-emerge as shrewdness. Kindness may re-emerge as wickedness.
8	人之迷也， 其日固久矣。	People are perplexed for a long time.
9	是以	Therefore,
10	方而不割， 廉而不刺， 直而不肆， 光而不耀。	Be square, but do not cut. [1] Be sharp, but do not pierce. Be straight, but do not be ruthless. Be bright, but do not bedazzle. [2]

---

[1] **58:10** This verse emphasizes the principles of inner discipline, despite the outer perplexities, because everything will follows its natural course. For example, we should maintain our squareness without cutting others, by adhering to the principle of Tao. We may be square inside without cutting others outside. 廉 means sharpness with edge.

[2] **58:10** Bedazzle is to shine brightly to temporarily blind others.

59 Support and Service 治人事天

1	治人事天 莫若嗇。	Managing people and serving heaven should be like farming.[1]
2	夫唯嗇， 是以早服，	As with farming, we submit (to nature) from the beginning.[2]
3	早服是謂 重積德。	Submission from the beginning leads to firm cultivation of Te.[3]
4	重積德 則無不克，	With firm cultivation of Te, there is nothing that it cannot overcome.
5	無不克 則莫知其極。	With nothing not overcome, it will prevail without a limit.
6	莫知其極， 可以有國；	Prevailing without a limit, it can be used to manage a country.
7	有國之母， 可以長久。	Managing a country with this principle will endure long.[4]
8	是謂	This is why we say:
9	深根固柢， 長生久視之道也。	Deep roots and firm principles are the way to ensure an enduring long life.[5]

---

[1] **59:1** Husbandry 嗇 is farming and frugal and sensitive management of resources. With great reserve.

[2] **59:2** 早服 Farmers are always prepared to submit to the nature. 早備.To prepare during the initiating stage. The initiating stage must be firm.

[3] **59:3** 重積德 means continuously or abundantly cultivation in Te. The result is a firm capacity to follow Te.

[4] **59:7** To have the mother of the country, 有國之母, means to have the fundamental principles for managing a country.

[5] **59:9** 久視 is a sustaining life.

60 Interweaving Te to Return 德交歸焉

1	治大邦 若烹小鮮。	Ruling a large state is like cooking a small fish.
2	以道蒞天下， 其鬼不神。	When Tao presides under heaven, its spirit remains un-manifested.[1]
3	非 其鬼不神也， 其神不傷人也。	Not just its spirit refrains from manifesting, but its manifestation will not interfere.[2]
4	非 其神不傷人也， 聖人亦弗傷也。	Not just its manifestation will not interfere, but Sage will also not interfere.
5	夫 兩不相傷， 故德交歸焉。	When these two do not interfere with each other, their Te's interweave and return (to Oneness).[3]

---

[1] **60:2** Our interpretation of spirit 鬼 and god 神 is discussed in Section 3.9 and 9.3. Spirit is the un-manifested (implicit) state of Tao. God 神 refers to the manifested (explicit) state of Tao. Spirit 鬼 is not ghost or demon, but is "the latent spirit" of Tao. God 神 is not a personalized god, but is Tao's discernable "manifestation or power."

[2] **60:3** 非 is a conjunction to indicate *Not* or *Not only*. 不傷人 Does not harm or interfere with nature.

[3] **60:7** The Two may refer to two Te's. The Te acts of the Sage and the Te acts of heaven will not interfere with each other. Both refer to the Yo state of heaven and of man that follow the same laws of interaction, which is Te. Therefore, the Te actions of the Sage will resonate with the Te actions of heaven (德交) to return to the state of Oneness with Tao.

61 A Great State stays Lower 大邦者下流

1 大邦者
   下流也。
   Large states are like
   the lowest reaches of a river.

2 天下之牝也，
   天下之交也。
   They are the source for all under heaven and
   the converging point for all under heaven. [1]

3 牝恒
   以靜勝牡。
   This (tender) source always
   overcome forces with tranquility. [2]

4 爲其靜也，
   故宜爲下。
   To maintain its tranquility,
   it prefers to stay low.

5 大邦以下小邦，
   則取小邦；
   A large state stays low towards the small states,
   as a way to win the small states.

6 小邦以下大邦，
   則取於大邦。
   A small state stays low towards the large state,
   as a way to win from the large state.

7 故或下以取，
   或下而取。
   Therefore, some stay low to win and
   some to win from. [3]

8 故
   大邦者不過
   欲兼畜人，
   Therefore,
   A large state should be without ambitions, and
   reach out to protect the people.

9 小邦者不過
   欲入事人，
   A small state should be without ambitions, and
   join in to serve the people.

10 夫皆得其欲，
   大者宜爲下。
   Each can get what it desires.
   The large ones should stay low.

---

[1] **61:2** 牝 is a female animal, the source of life for all under heaven. See Chapter 6. Here this also refers to the function of a large state to support the small states. The large state is also 天下之交 the converging point for all under heaven. 牝 is also used in Chapter 6.

[2] **61:3** 牡 is a male animal, which represents strength or the forceful one.

[3] **61:7** In Wentzu 文子道德篇: When a strong country has Tao, it will win without wars 強大有道，不戰而克; when a weak country has Tao, it will gain without struggles 小弱有道，不爭而得.

62 Lord of All-Beings 萬物之主

1	道者萬物之主也。	Tao is the lord of all beings. It is
2	善人之寶也，	a treasure for whoever can master it, and
	不善人之所保也。	a redeemer for whoever cannot master it.
3	美言可以市，	(Even) smart words can gain respect and
	尊行可以加人；	fine behaviors can impress people.
4	人之不善，	If people can not master (Tao),
	何棄之有。	how can we just abandon them?
5	故	Therefore,
	立天子，	the Son of Heaven is enthroned, and
	置三卿。	three ministers are installed. [1]
6	雖有拱之璧	Although endowed with respect, and
	以駟駟馬，	chartered with power, they are
7	不若坐而進此。	not as good as to sit to enter into Tao. [2]
8	古之所以貴此者，	The ancient treasure this Tao;
	何也？不謂	why? Not other than this:
9	求以得，	If we seek, we will attain (Tao);
	有罪以免與，	our mishaps will be eradicated. [3]
10	故為	Therefore, it is
	天下貴。	the treasure of all under heaven.

---

[1] **62:5** The son of heaven is to mediate between man and heaven, so Tao can reach the people through him. Three ministers are installed to teach people.

[2] **62:7** We have taken the literal translation of 進此 "to enter into this" as "to enter into Tao." The same interpretation is used in Verse 8 for 貴此者 as to treasure this Tao.

[3] **62:9** If Tao is sought, it will be attained (以求得) and all sins will be forgiven.

63 Act with Wu-Actions 爲無爲

1	爲無爲，	Act with Wu-actions.
	事無事，	Conduct with Wu-efforts.
	味無味。	Taste the tasteless.
2	大小多少，	Large or small, many or few, we should
	報怨以德。	respond to all adversaries with Te. [1]
3	圖難乎	To attack a difficult task,
	其易也，	we look into its easy subtasks.
	爲大乎	To plan a large task,
	其細也。	we look into its small subtasks.
4	天下之難	All difficult tasks under heaven can be
	作於易，	accomplished via their easy subtasks.
5	天下之大	All large tasks under heaven can be
	作於細。	accomplished via their small subtasks.
6	是以聖人	This is why the Sage
7	終不爲大，	never takes on a large task (directly), so
	故能成其大。	he can accomplish his large tasks.
8	夫	Because,
	輕諾必寡信，	Quick promises have little trustworthiness.
	多易必多難。	Presumed easiness will lead to difficulties. [2]
9	是以	This is why
	聖人猶難之，	the Sage prepares for difficulties, so
	故終於無難。	he can accomplish without difficulty. [3]

---

[1] **63:2** Respond to any resentment or difficult situation with the proper attitudes prescribed by Te. In Wentzu 文子: In Tao of Heaven and earth, large is based on small and many begin with few 天地之道，大以小爲本，多以少爲始。

[2] **63:8** Assuming a main task itself as easy will lead to many difficulties. If one takes too many tasks as easy, one may err in attacking the task without preparation.

[3] **63:9** Hesitate with caution 猶難. Sage acts with hesitation because he is aware of potential difficulties. To be prepared for difficulties. Hang in doubt.

64　Sustain with Stability 其安易持

1	其安也，易持也。 其未兆也，易謀也。	While stable, it is easy to sustain. While latent, it is easy to plan.
2	其脆也，易破也。 其微也，易散也。	While fragile, it is easy to break up. While small, it is easy to disperse.
3	爲之於其未有也， 治之於其未亂也。	Act on it before it is manifested. Manage it before it becomes chaotic.
4	合抱之木， 生於毫末；	An armful-sized large tree starts from a small tip.
5	九層之臺， 作於虆土；	A nine-storied pavilion builds from a dirt pile.
6	百仞之高， 始於足下。	A height of 700 feet [1] begins with a footstep.
7	爲之者敗之， 執之者失之。	Acting otherwise causes failure. Steering otherwise causes deviation. [2]

(Chapter 64 continues next page.)

---

[1] **64:6** 仞 is a unit of seven feet.

[2] **64:7** This verse also appears in Verse 29:4. The literal translation is "acting on the above process will cause failure" and "steering on the above process will cause deviations."

8	是以聖人	Therefore, the Sage
9	無爲也，故無敗也；	Acts with Wu, so he never fails.
	無執也，故無失也。	Steers with Wu, so he never deviates.
10	民之從事也，	People, in conducting their work, often
	恒於幾成而敗之。	fail when goals are nearly achieved.[1]
11	故慎終如始，	Watch at the end, as in the beginning,
	則無敗事矣。	will lead to no failure.
12	是以聖人	Therefore, the Sage
13	欲不欲，	seeks no desire, so
	而不貴難得之貨；	he does not cherish rare goods;[2]
14	學不學，	learns to unlearn, so he can
	而復眾人之所過。	return from what others have erred.
15	能輔萬物之自然，	To support the nature of all beings,
	而弗敢爲。	he dares not taking his own actions.

---

[1] **64:10** This verse refers to the concept of returning to Wu when a full Yo state is reached. If this step of returning is not properly executed, it will become a failure (by overflowing.).

[2] **64:13** A Sage would let the accomplishment (as rare goods) go.

65　The Greatest Harmony 大順

1	故曰：	So we say:
2	爲道者 非以明民也， 將以愚之也。	The one with Tao is not to brighten up the people, but to keep them in simplicity.[1]
3	夫民之難治也， 以其智也。	People are hard to manage, because the ruler relies on his knowledge.[2]
4	故以智治國， 國之賊也；	Therefore, governing a state with knowledge is a disservice to the state.
5	不以智治國， 國之德也。	Governing a state not with knowledge is a blessing to the state.
6	恆知此兩者， 亦稽式也。	Knowing the distinction of these two is an important guiding rule.
7	恒知稽式， 此謂玄德。	Knowing this guiding rule is known as the Heavenly Te.[3]
8	玄德深矣， 遠矣，與物反矣， 乃至大順。	This Heavenly Te reaches deep, ranges far, and reverts with all to the Greatest Harmony.

---

[1] **65:2** The one who acts with Tao 爲道者 is qualified as a ruler or leader, so he is expected to act with Wu (wisdom), and not to act with Yo (knowledge). A coherent interpretation of 愚之 is to keep the people in a simple state of mind, as though a fool (in the state of Pu). See also verse **20:10**, and Section 5.4.

[2] **65:3** The word zhi 智 refers to temporary worldly knowledge. A ruler should rule with Wu and not with Yo, as also stated in Verse **48:4** and **75:2**. It does not mean true wisdom; the true wisdom is Wu-wisdom. See Section 4.4.

[3] **65:7** This chapter emphasizes the importance of ruling by Wu; the law of interaction in the Wu state is called Heavenly Te 玄德. This is also discussed in verse **10:8**.

66   All Valleys will Follow 百谷王

1	江海所以能爲 百谷王者，	The rivers and the seas can be where all valleys home to, [1] because
2	以其善下之， 是以能爲百谷王。	they know how to stay low, to let all valleys home to them.
3	是以	Similarly,
4	聖人之欲上民也， 必以其言下之；	The Sage wishes to lift the people, so he keeps his words humble;
5	其欲先民也， 必以其身後之。	He wishes to lead the people, so he puts himself behind the people.
6	故居前 而民弗害也，	Therefore, when he is in the front, the people encounter no hindrance.
7	居上 而民弗重也。	When he is above, the people feel no burden.
8	天下皆樂推 而弗厭也。	All under heaven are happy to support him with no resentment.
9	不以其無爭與， 故天下莫能與爭。	He never contends, so nothing under heaven can contend against him.

---

[1] **66:1** 百谷王 may be literally translated as the king of one-hundred valleys. 王 represents something that all under heaven will follow, or something that encompasses all under heaven. It is the controlling force on all valleys, and the valleys will naturally seek out, follow, and flow to the rivers and the seas. 王 is also used in Verses **16:11**.and **25:9**.

67   Three Treasures 三寶

1	天下皆謂我大， 大而不肖。	All under heaven claim that Tao is immense.[1] It is great and does not resemble anything.
2	夫唯不肖， 故能大；	Because it does not resemble anything, it can be immense.
3	若肖， 久矣其細也夫。	If it resembles anything, it will eventually become small (fragmented).
4	我恒有三寶， 持而寶之。	Tao always hold three treasures to preserve its immenseness.[2]
5	一曰慈， 二曰儉，三曰 不敢爲天下先。	The first is compassion. The second is prudence. The third is not to stand ahead of others.
6	夫慈故能勇； 儉故能廣； 不敢爲天下先， 故能爲成事長。	With compassion, it may have courage. With prudence, it can reach broadly. By not standing ahead of others, it can support others to develop.
8	今	Now.
9	捨其慈，且勇； 捨其儉，且廣； 捨其後，且先；	We discard compassion, to seek courage. We discard prudence, to seek broadness. We discard the rear, to seek the front.
10	則必死矣。	We will perish!
11	夫慈，	With compassion,
12	以戰則勝， 以守則固。	it will triumph in offense and it will withstand in defense.
13	天將建之， 如以慈垣之。	Whatever heaven wants to erect, heaven will protect it with compassion.[3]

---

[1] **67:1** We interpret 我, as Tao; instead of a literal translation of I. For immenseness, see Chapter 25.

[2] **67:4** There are three ways to keep Tao immense and not to resemble anything.

[3] **67:13** All-encompassing nature is the basic support for Tao. We may interpret this to mean that Compassion is the most important aspect of Tao and is also stated in Verse 10 of Chapter 25.

68 Conforming to Heaven 用人配天

1	故	So.
	善爲士者不武，	Skillful strategists show no belligerence. [1]
2	善戰者不怒，	Capable warriors show no anger.
3	善勝敵者弗與；	Clever conquerors never engage (in a war). [2]
4	善用人者爲之下。	Competent leaders stay low.
5	是謂不爭之德，	It is the Te of Non-contention.
6	是謂用人，	It is the way to lead people. [3]
7	是謂配天，	It is the way to conform to heaven.
8	古之極也。	This is the ultimate of all ages.

---

[1] **68:1** Huainantzu 淮南子: Those who are good at administration cultivate their Te 善爲政者積其德; Those who are good at warfare conceal their anger 善用兵者畜其怒

[2] **68:3** Huainantzu 淮南子: winning armies win before going to the war 王兵先勝而後戰, Losing armies start a war then seek to win 敗兵先戰而後求勝, This is because they do not understand Tao 此不明於道」

[3] **68:6** 用人 is to make use of the strength of others.

69 War Motto 用兵有言

1	用兵有言曰：	There is a motto for war:
2	吾不敢爲主而爲客；	Don't be a host; stay as a guest.
3	不敢進寸而退尺。	Don't advance an inch; retreat a foot.
4	是謂	This is known as:
	行無行，	marching without formations,
5	攘無臂，	repelling without arms,
6	執無兵，	engaging without armies, and
7	乃無敵矣。	confronting without animosity.
8	禍莫大於	The most disastrous is
	無敵，	to brave the enemy.[1]
9	無敵	Braving the enemy will
	近亡吾寶矣。	ruin our treasures (of Tao).[2]
10	故	Therefore.
11	稱兵相若，	When the armies are engaged,
	則哀者勝矣。	the one with compassion will triumph.[3]

---

[1] **69:8** 無敵, *braving the enemy*, may have two related interpretations. It may first mean to look down on the enemy and to engage in a war lightly, that is, to take an enemy lightly. Another interpretation is to use the courage and force to eliminate the enemy. It is clear for overall coherency in this chapter, *braving the enemy* should mean "to use courage and force to defeat an enemy." This is also echoed in Chapter 67, where Laotzu states that we often try to rely on courage without compassion.

[2] **69:9** The three treasures are in Chapter 67.

[3] **69:11** 哀者 is often interpreted as sorrow or gravity. We agree with Wang Bi's comment on this as "compassion." This verse is linked to verses 8 and 8, and the compassion discussed in Chapter 67, for coherency.

70   My Teachings are Easy 吾言甚易知

1	吾言甚易知也， 甚易行也。	My teaching is very easy to understand, and very easy to practice.
2	而人 莫之能知也， 莫之能行也。	But people cannot understand it and cannot practice it.
3	言有宗， 事有君。	All teachings have their principles. All efforts have their guiding rules.
4	夫唯無知也， 是以不我知。	Unless with Wu-wisdom,[1] there is no way to understand my principles.
5	知我者希， 則我貴矣。	Few have understood my principles. Even fewer have followed my principles.
6	是以聖人	This is like a Sage
7	被褐而裹玉。	wearing drabness and hiding jades inside.[2]

---

[1] **70:4** 無知 is the ultimate wisdom associated with the Wu state. See Section 3.13.

[2] **70:7** The reason that Tao is hard to recognize is that it is concealed within something very ordinary. The Tao appears ordinary or raggedy outside, but it holds real valuables to the chest inside.

151

71   Wisdom of Ignorance 知不知

1   知不知，尚矣；   Wisdom about ignorance is an honor.[1]
2   不知知，病矣。   Ignorance about wisdom is sickness.[2]
3   是以聖人之不病。   But the Sage shows no such sickness.[3]
4   以其病病，   He is sick of all sicknesses, so
    是以不病。   he has no sickness.

---

[1] **71:1** To be wise 知 about ignorance 不知 is honored. In Chuangtzu Chapter 2, we have, "To stop at what one does not know is the ultimate wisdom. 故知止 其所不知，至矣。"

[2] **71:2** To be ignorant 不知 about Wisdom 知 is a sickness 病. We often think something is good and something else is sick, but this attitude itself is sick in Tao philosophy. This is shown in Verse 3.

[3] **71:3** Sickness 病 is used as a noun or a verb. This verse indicates that a Sage will not take either proclamations in verses 1 and 2. He would not make judgment on Verse 1 or Verse 2; either one is a sickness. Laotzu also emphasizes this positive attitude also prominently in Chapter 27 (Verses 7 and 8), Chapter 49 (Verses 2 and 4), and Chapter 72 (Verse 3).

72 Greatest Authority can enter 大威將至

1	民之不畏威，	When people have no fear for the authority,
	則大威將至矣。	the Greatest Authority can enter. [1]
2	毋狎	It (Tao) shows no dislike
	其所居，	towards where people live.
	毋厭	It shows no dislike
	其所生。	towards how people live.
3	夫唯弗厭，	Only by showing no dislike,
	是以不厭。	it will not be disliked. [2]
4	是以聖人	This is why the Sage retains
5	自知	self-wisdom
	而不自見也，	without displaying it, and
	自愛	self-respect
	而不自貴也。	without extolling it. [3]
6	故去彼取此。	He would not want it any other way.

---

[1] **72:1** The Greatest Authority 大威 refers to Tao or the Sage. It follows that the Sage should not create any fear of Tao or himself, so the people can accept the true Tao or his interactions, without fear or dislike.淮南泰族:「不言而信,不施而仁,不怒而威,是以天心動化者也」

[2] **72:3** Like Tao, a Sage will not show his dislike towards people, so people will not reject him.

[3] **72:5** To have wisdom for oneself, but not to display wisdom to glorify oneself. Otherwise he will invoke ill feeling among the people, before they can let his teachings into their hearts.文子:「君子之道,靜以修身,儉以養生.靜即下不擾,下不擾即民不怨」

73   Net of Heaven 天網恢恢

1	勇於敢者則殺， 勇於不敢者則活。

1   勇於敢者則殺，   To be brave and daring will perish.
     勇於不敢者則活。   To be brave but not daring will survive.
2   此兩者   Of these two,
     或利或害。   which is good and which is bad?
3   天之所惡，   Whatever heaven dislikes we really
     孰知其故？   do not know the reason for.
4   天之道，   The Tao of Heaven always
5   不戰而善勝，   overcomes without contention,
6   不言而善應，   responds without words, and
7   不召而自來，   comes without invitation.
8   坦而善謀。   Tao protects and plans well. [1]
9   天網恢恢，   The net of heaven is imperceptible.
     疏而不失。   Its meshes are loose,
                        but nothing slips through it. [2]

---

[1] **73:8** We choose to adopt the same interpretation for 坦 as *to protect*, as in Chapter 67. We make the subject of the sentence explicit as Tao.

[2] **73:9** We may say that, "Nothing can escape through its loose meshes."

74   **Unafraid of Death** 民不畏死

1   若民恒且不畏死，
     奈何以殺懼之也？

If people are unafraid of death,[1]
why threaten them with death?

2   若民恒且畏死，
     而爲奇者，
     吾得而殺之，

If people are afraid of death and
behave as rebels,[2]
we capture and kill them.

3   夫孰敢矣。

But, how dare we?

4   若民恒且必畏死，
     則恒有司殺者。

If people must face death,
there is already an Executioner.[3]

5   夫代司殺者殺，
     是代大匠斲也。

To kill for this Executioner is
to pretend as a master craftsman.

6   夫代大匠斲者，
     則希
     不傷其手矣。

Whoever pretends as a master
craftsman can seldom avoid
injuring his own hands.

---

[1] **74:1** 恒且 seems to carry a meaning of "if" and assumption.

[2] **74:2** 奇 is deviation. 奇者 is a rebel, non-conformant, or a strange person.

[3] **74:4** The Executioner is the natural course for life and death.

155

75 Abundant Life 賢貴生

1	人之饑也， 以其取食稅之多也， 是以饑。	People starve because the ruler levies too much grain-tax to make them starve.
2	百姓之不治也， 以其上之有以爲也， 是以不治。	People are hard to manage because the ruler acts with Yo, so he cannot manage.[1]
3	民之輕死， 以其求生之厚也， 是以輕死。	(But) people take their lives lightly, because they seek abundance in life. This makes them take their lives lightly.[2]
4	夫唯 無以生爲者， 是賢貴生。	Therefore, only those who live by Wu are able to have an abundant life.[3]

---

[1] **75:2** The ruler (上) acts with Yo (有爲), instead of Wu. The message is that if a ruler cannot act with Wu, he is unfit to rule [**48:05**]. In Chuangtzu Chapter 13: The ruler must act with Wu to guide under heaven; the people must act with Yo to be useful under heaven 上必無爲而用天下，下必有爲爲天下用。 See also Verse **65:3**.

[2] **75:3** We may also interpret this verse to mean that the people seek too much luxury in their lives, so they end up taking their lives lightly. Verses 1 and 2 refer to the actions of the ruler, but this verse refers to the action taken by the people.

[3] **75:4** 無以生 is to rely on Wu to live, or to live by the spirit of the Wu-state and according to Tao. Also used in Chapter 39. 貴生 is taken to mean a life of honor and value.

76   Tenderness for Life 柔弱生之徒

1	人之生也柔弱， 其死也筋肕堅強。	Birth of a man is tender and soft. His death is hard and stiff. [1]
2	萬物草木之生 也柔脆， 其死也枯槁。	Birth of all beings and plants is tender and delicate. Their deaths are dry and brittle.
3	故曰： 堅強者死之徒也， 柔弱者生之徒也。	So we may say: The hard and stiff leads to death. The tender and soft leads to life. [2]
4	是以	For this reason,
5	兵強則不勝， 木強則烘。	Armies showing strength will not win. Trees showing strength are cut for fire. [3]
6	強大居下， 柔弱居上。	Being strong is not preferred. [4] Being tender is preferred.

---

[1] **76:1** 人之生 The life of man or the birth of man.

[2] **76:3** 生之徒 refers to the agent for life or the way to support life. The one who can survive.

[3] **76:5** 烘 is to burn or cut for fire. In Lie Tzu, we have: Armies showing strength will be terminated 兵強則滅。

[4] **76:6** 居下 is to be less desirable. To be treated with disadvantage. To be considered inferior.

77 The Way of Heaven 天之道

1	天之道， 猶張弓者也!	The way of heaven is like the way we string a bow.
2	高者抑之， 下者舉之；	The higher is bent down and the lower is pulled up.
3	有餘者損之， 不足者補之。	Slack is tautened and strain is slackened.
4	故天之道， 損有餘 而補不足；	Therefore, the way of heaven is to take from the surplus and add to the shortfall.
5	人之道則不然， 損不足 而奉有餘。	The way of man is not so. It takes from the shortfall and add to the surplus.
6	孰能有餘而 有以取奉於天者乎？	How can we learn enough and can follow heaven? [1]
7	唯有道者乎。	Only those who follow Tao can.
8	是以聖人	Therefore, the Sage
9	爲而弗有， 成功而弗居也，	acts without showing his efforts, and accomplishes without occupying.
10	若此 其不欲見賢也。	By this, he has no intention to display his wealth (capacity). [2]

---

[1] **77:6** How can we avoid the way of man and build enough capacity and follow the way of Tao to serve the world? Huainantzu 淮南子: 能者有餘，拙者不足. 無欲則有餘，有欲則不瞻也已.

[2] **77:10** The word 見 is to display and 賢 is wealth, as noted in [CH00]. See Section 9.5. A Sage will not accumulate to show his surplus capacity or plentiful-ness, but everything is properly done.

78 Easiness made with Wu 無以易之

1	天下 莫柔弱於水，	Under heaven, nothing is softer than water.
2	而攻堅強者 莫之能勝也，	But, to attack a stronghold, nothing else works better.
3	以其 無以易之也。	Because of its ability to make things easy with its Wu nature.[1]
4	柔之勝剛， 弱之勝強，	The soft will overcome the hard. The weak will overcome the strong.[2]
5	天下莫弗知也， 莫能行也。	All under heaven know this, but are unable to practice it.
6	故聖人之言云， 曰：	Therefore, the Sage would say this:
7	「受邦之垢， 是謂社稷之主； 受邦之不祥， 是謂 天下之王。」	"Bearing (small) disgraces for the state, one may become a provincial lord. Bearing (great) misfortune for the state, one may become what all under heaven will follow."[3]
8	正言若反。	The right teaching seems reversed.

---

[1] **78:3** Uses its Wu-nature (以其無) to make it easy (以易之). Water makes the task easy by its nature of Wu.

[2] **78:4** Making it weak is better than making it strong; Making it soft is better than making it hard.

[3] **78:7** Whoever stays humble or weak, as though bearing the disgrace of the country, can best serve as a small lord. The most humble or the weakest, as though the most disgraced, one may serve as the supreme lord that all under heaven will follow.

79   Settling a Great Animosity 和大怨

1	和大怨， 必有餘怨。	After settling a great animosity, some resentments certainly remain.
2	焉可以爲善？	How is this settled?
3	是以聖人	For this, the Sage will
4	執右契， 而不以責於人。	tender the right contract[1] and blame not on others.
5	故 有德司契， 無德司徹。	Because, the one with Te will offer, and the one without Te will demand.[2]
6	夫天道無親， 恒與善人。	Since the Way of Heaven is impartial, it always stays with the kind one.

---

[1] **79:4** We have followed Mawangdui Text A, which has 右契. (Mawangdui Text set B has 左契.) The right side of the contract 右契 specifies what the holder needs to deliver; the left portion specifies what the holder will get. This interpretation is consistent with the ancient convention that right side is the place of humbleness.

[2] **79:5** Wentzu 文子: When Chi is in harmony, one sacrifices to serve others 氣順則自損以奉人，when Chi is against harmony, one sacrifices others to serve oneself 氣逆則損人以自奉。

80   Small states with few people 小邦寡民

1	小邦寡民。	In a small state with few people:
2	使有十百人之器 而毋用；	There is heavy equipment, [1] but is unused.
3	使民重死 而遠徙。	People value their lives dearly and avoid venturing far. [2]
4	有舟車 無所乘之；	There are boats and carriages, but are unused for journeys.
5	有甲兵 無所陳之；	There are armors and soldiers, [3] but are not displayed.
6	使民 復結繩而用之。	The people return to making and using tie-knots.
7	甘其食， 美其服，	They enjoy their food and smarten their wear,
8	樂其俗， 安其居。	They are happy with what they believe, and are content with where they live.
9	鄰邦相望， 雞狗之聲相聞，	Other countries are close by. Chickens and dogs can be heard.
10	民至老死 不相往來。	People live till old and die, with no need to cross the borders.

---

[1] **80:2** Heavy equipment that can handle workload of ten 十 or hundred 百 persons.

[2] **80:3** 重死 is treat death as a grave matter and will avoid death by not taking risk on their life, as opposed to live lightly as in Light Death (輕死) [75.03]. 遠徙 is to travel far 徙 and become separated 遠.

[3] **80:5** 甲兵 are armors and soldiers.

81 Trustworthy Teachings 信言不美

1	信言不美， 美言不信。	Trustworthy teachings are undecorated. Decorated teachings are not trustworthy.
2	知者不博， 博者不知。	Whoever has wisdom is not boastful. [1] Whoever is boastful has no wisdom.
3	善者不多， 多者不善。	Whoever has mastered does not show a lot. [2] Whoever shows a lot has not mastered.
4	聖人無積，	The Sage does not accrue (for himself).
5	既以爲人， 己愈有； 既以予人矣， 己愈多。	Only by doing more for others, he receives more. Only by giving more to others, he gains more.
6	故天之道， 利而不害；	The Tao of Heaven is to support without hindrance.
7	人之道， 爲而弗爭。	The Tao of man is to act without contention.

---

[1] **81:2** Whoever has wisdom will not boast about his abundance of wisdom. Boasting of knowledge is often a cover-up for lack of wisdom. In Chuangtzu Chapter 16: Boasting drowns our minds 博溺心。

[2] **81:3** Whoever has mastered Tao 善者 will not accumulate or show abundance of his wisdom. Wang Bi version has 不辯 instead of 不多, which may also indicate that when wisdom is accumulated and shown, it may lead to debates. Chuangtzu Chapter 2: A Sage will discuss, but not debate 聖人論而不辯, Greatest Debate uses any word 大辯不言, and Debate using no word. 不言之辯。

INDEX